MILITARY HISTORY
FROM PRIMARY SOURCES

RENAISSANCE WARFARE

JAMES GRANT

EDITED AND INTRODUCED
BY BOB CARRUTHERS

Pen & Sword
MILITARY

This edition published in 2013 by
Pen & Sword Military
An imprint of
Pen & Sword Books Ltd
47 Church Street
Barnsley
South Yorkshire
S70 2AS

First published in Great Britain in 2012 in digital format by
Coda Books Ltd.

ISBN 978 1 78159 230 4

This book contains an extract from 'British Battles on Land and Sea'
by James Grant. Published by Cassell and Company Limited, 1894.

Printed and bound in Great Britain
by CPI Group (UK) Ltd, Croydon, CR0 4YY

Pen & Sword Books Ltd incorporates the Imprints of Pen & Sword Aviation, Pen
& Sword Family History, Pen & Sword Maritime, Pen & Sword Military, Pen
& Sword Discovery, Pen & Sword Politics, Pen & Sword Atlas, Pen & Sword
Archaeology, Wharncliffe Local History, Wharncliffe True Crime, Wharncliffe
Transport, Pen & Sword Select, Pen & Sword Military Classics, Leo Cooper, The
Praetorian Press, Claymore Press, Remember When, Seaforth Publishing and
Frontline Publishing

For a complete list of Pen & Sword titles please contact
PEN & SWORD BOOKS LIMITED
47 Church Street, Barnsley, South Yorkshire, S70 2AS, England
E-mail: enquiries@pen-and-sword.co.uk
Website: www.pen-and-sword.co.uk

CONTENTS

INTRODUCTION
BY BOB CARRUTHERS

THIS REMARKABLE work features a comprehensive survey of the defining events of warfare in the British Isles as described by the great Victorian military writer James Grant. The modern reader seeking an insight into the military events of the Renaissance era need look no further than the excellent work of Mr. Grant. I had the pleasure to revise and edit the text for publication and I was impressed by Mr. Grant's outstanding scholarship, his extraordinary depth of knowledge and also by his sympathetic understanding which allowed me to gain an insight into the tremendous research he had conducted into his subject which will deepen the reader's understanding of an absorbing piece of British history.

Originally published as part of the Cassell's Series "*British Battles on Land and Sea*" it presents the reader with an intriguing insight into how key Victorian writers addressed their subject. They say the past is another country and that is certainly true in this instance. The contrast between the contemporary Victorian view and the modern view reveals the huge gulf in attitudes. Mr. Grant's work is clearly 'of its time' and reflects the attitudes of the day which were unashamedly xenophobic, jingoistic and militaristic. It nonetheless repays the reader as it provides us with a unique window on the past and brings the long lost world of Victorian values into focus.

The engravings and illustrations are late nineteenth century and are reproduced as close as possible to how they originally appeared in the pages of "*British Battles on Land and Sea*". The works of imagination depicting the key events from the thick of the action are fairly obviously embroidered and romanticised, but the portraits, landscapes and depictions of everyday soldiering all have a period flavour. These wonderful engravings provide a direct link with the past and together with Mr. Grant's period text produce an absorbing account of the renaissance warfare through Victorian eyes.

- C H A P T E R   I -

FLODDEN, 1513

IT CAME to pass now, by the turn of events and of the times, that the same Earl of Surrey who in 1503 had handed to James IV of Scotland his royal and beautiful English bride, at Lamberton Kirk, in the Merse, was destined to be his opponent and conqueror, ten years afterwards, in that battle which was so disastrous to Scotland, and was long remembered as a calamity so great that its name still recalls something of sadness; for there was scarcely a family of importance which was not bereaved of a husband, a father, a brother, or a son. In some instances all the males of a family perished side by side, fighting for their king and country.

Though war had been ostensibly declared by the King of Scotland to aid his ally, the King of France, it was undoubtedly accelerated by the brawls and raids of the borderers. Shortly before the declaration, Sir Robert Kerr, of Cessford, Warden of the Middle Marches, had been run through by a lance and dispatched by Sir William Heron, Lilburn, and Starkhed, three English borderers. Henry VIII gave up Lilburn to the Scots, but Starkhed for the time escaped. The former was sent a prisoner to Fast Castle, with Heron of Ford, a brother of the murderer, and died there; but Andrew Kerr, son of the slain knight, killed Starkhed, and placed his head on one of the gates of Edinburgh; and then followed the sea-fight with Barton, and many other causes of irritation, among which, the mean manner in which Henry VIII absolutely cheated his sister, the Scottish queen, out of her father's legacy, was perhaps one. Yet the war was not popular with the mass of the Scottish people. However, the king was so beloved by his subjects of all ranks, that when orders were given to assemble the army of the realm on the Burgh

Muir of Edinburgh, then the Campus Martius of the Scottish hosts, the appeal was responded to by the muster of one of the best-equipped armies that as yet Scotland had ever seen.

La Motte, the French Ambassador, brought the king a ring from the finger of Anne of Bretagne, Queen of France, and a letter, written in an amorous strain, appealing to his chivalry, terming him her own knight, and beseeching him to advance only three steps on English ground, with his army, for the sake of her who considered him her defender. It was in vain that the wisest of his counsellors sought to dissuade James from war, and that his queen, with sobs, tears, and caresses, implored him not to peril his own life by taking the field against Henry her brother; asking him, touchingly, "why he preferred the Queen of France to her, his wife, the mother of his children, whom he had wedded in her girlhood?"

But James, says Pitscottie, turned a deaf ear to all; so an attempt was made to dissuade him from his expedition, by working upon the emotions of superstitious melancholy which, partly from constitution, and partly from remorse for his rebellion against his unhappy father, formed a prominent feature in his character. The story of this device is related with great minuteness by Lindesay of Pitscottie, probably on the information of Sir David Lindesay, of the Mount, the Lyon King of Arms, then a very young man, who was present.

In St. Catherine's Aisle of the Chapel Royal of Linlithgow (now a parish church), where the king had constructed a throne for himself, with twelve stalls for the Knights of the Thistle, when he was engaged at his devotions there entered by the door a man of strange and solemn' aspect, clad in a blue weed, belted with a piece of linen. His forehead was bald; long yellow hair flowed upon his shoulders; he held in his right hand a long pilgrim's staff, and seemed to be about fifty years of age. Approaching the desk where James was kneeling at vesper prayer amid the gloom of the evening, "Sir king," said he, gravely and solemnly, "my mother hath sent me to thee, desiring thee not to pass at this time where thou art purposed, for if thou dost, thou wilt not fare well in thy journey, nor any who pass with thee. Further, she bade thee meddle with no woman, nor use their counsel, nor let them touch thy body, or thou theirs, for, if thou dost, thou shalt be confounded and put to shame."

Then, adds the chronicler, he vanished away, and slipped through the hands of those who sought to seize him, "as if he had been a blink of the sun or a whiff of the whirlwind, and could no more be seen."

The common belief in Scotland is that the whole was a device of Margaret Tudor to deter the king from war. This is made more apparent by the warning given concerning women, as she had good cause to be jealous of his love intrigues; and the phrase, "My mother sent me," was adopted to make James suppose his spectral monitor was the adopted son of Mary, St.

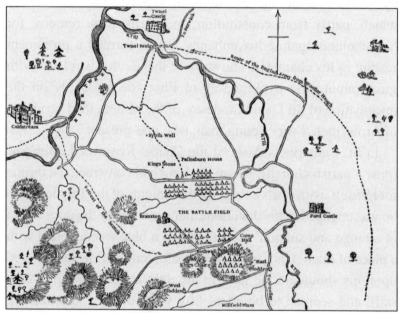

Plan of Flodden Field.

John the Evangelist. But prudence, superstition, and caresses proved unavailing. As Margaret had come to him without her father's legacy to preserve her from pecuniary embarrassments, James gave her an order on his treasury for 180,000 crowns, and took his departure for the camp. The high turret in Linlithgow Palace, so well known to tourists as Queen Margaret's Bower, is said to be the place where she retired to weep, and watch the departure of that fated monarch who was to return no more.

On the Burgh Muir of Edinburgh, a place then, according to Hawthornden, delightful by the shade of many stately oaks, he met the feudal array of Scotland, and planted his royal standard in the Hare Stone, a large block, a portion of which still remains by the highway leading to Braid, and now becoming a street. There assembled the whole nobility, barons, and burgesses of the realm, "between sixty and sixteen, spiritual and temporal, burgh and land, islesmen and others," to the number of 100,000 men (a force which subsequently diminished), under their chiefs, the male adults of every family, capable of bearing arms, except the eldest son, an order founded on the assumption that if all the others of the family were cut off, he would maintain the females and junior members.

Every man had with him provisions for forty days, and all were arrayed according to Act of Parliament passed in 1491, which ordained that every possessor of ten pounds' worth of land or more shall have a helmet or salade, gorget or pisane, and mail for the limbs, a sword, spear, and dagger. "All other yeomen of the realm, betwixt sextie and sextene, sail have sufficient bowes and sheaves, sword, buckler, knife, speare, or ane gude axe instead of a bow;" adding that every man, according to his means, must be accoutred in "white harness" or good jacks, with gloves of plate, and well-horsed, correspondent to his lands and goods." The Scots were then famous for the temper of their sword-blades. "A great armourer arose in the Highlands," says

Smiles, in his "Industrial Biography," "one who was able to forge armour that would resist the best Sheffield arrow-heads, and to make swords that would vie with the best weapons of Toledo and Milan."

This was the great cutler, Andrea de Ferrara, whose swords still maintain their ancient reputation. He is supposed to have learned his art in .the Italian city whence he was called, and, under the patronage of the King of Scotland, to have practised it in secrecy among the Highland hills, as all his genuine blades are marked with a crown; and before his time no man in Great Britain could temper a sword in such a way that the point should touch the hilt and spring back uninjured. He is said to have worked in a dark cellar, the better to enable him to perceive the effect of the heat upon the metal, and to watch the nicety of the tempering; as well as possibly to serve as a screen to his secret method of working. Many of his blades, with new basket hilts, are to be found in the Scottish regiments of the present day.

James had with him a very efficient train of thirty pieces of artillery, which had been cast for him at Edinburgh by the master gunner of the castle there, Robert Borthwick, who was also a bell-founder. Seven of these were guns of great beauty, which were known as the "Seven Sisters of Borthwick." As these cannon were being brought forth in the night, a strange cry was heard at the cross of the city, known in Scottish history as "The Summons of Platcock" (or Pluto), and supposed to have been another ruse of the king's friends to prevent his march into England, as every "earl and lord, baron and gentlemen," in the army was required by name to appear in the world to come within forty days. "Whether," says Pitscottie, "this summons was proclaimed by vain persons, night walkers, or drunk men for their pastime, or if it was a spirit, I cannot tell;' but every man whose name was uttered, save one who heard his own given, and appealed to God against the summons, he adds, was slain at Flodden.

King James began his march for England at the head of one of the most formidable armies that had ever invaded it; and on the 22nd of August he crossed the Tweed, and encamped on the banks of the Till, near Twisel, where the army remained two days. Then marching down Tweed-side, he captured Norham, Wark, Etal, and Ford, four border castles, but these petty enterprises were only a waste of the time, provisions, and ammunition that should have enabled him to march to Newcastle. When Ford was stormed, Lady Heron, the wife of Sir William Heron, the castellan, who was still a prisoner in Scotland for the murder of the Laird of Cessford, was taken by James; and, according to the Scottish historians, this beautiful and artful dame had such influence over the infatuated monarch, as to induce him to idle away his time till his forces began to dwindle, and the opportunity for striking an effective blow was irretrievably lost.

While he lay thus inactive, his army suffering the while from scarcity of provisions and incessant rains, and, by the desertion of many Islemen and Highlanders, reduced to 30,000 men and the personal attendants of the knights and nobles, the army of England was mustering, under Thomas Howard, the Earl of Surrey. To him, during his absence, Henry had committed the defence of England, and he was now busy in Yorkshire, concentrating the military array of the northern counties, amounting to 26,000 men. In passing through Durham, he received from the prior of the convent there the sacred banner of St. Cuthbert, for the purpose of inspiring the courage of his soldiers. On the 30th of August he was joined at Newcastle by Thomas, Lord Dacre, of Gillesland, K.G; Sir William Bulmer, of Burnspeth Castle; Sir Marmaduke Constable, and others of the northern chivalry; and on reaching Alnwick was met by his son, Thomas, High Admiral of England, with a reinforcement of 5,000 well-trained soldiers from the English army in France. Nor should we forget worthy John Winchcombe, better known as Jack of Newbury, one of the greatest clothiers in England, who marched with 100 of his workmen, armed and equipped at his own expense, against the invaders. After this, Surrey finding himself the stronger of the two by more than 1,000 men, on the 4th of September sent a herald to challenge the Scottish king to fight a pitched battle on the following Friday, "if he had courage to remain so long on English ground."

Thomas, Lord Howard, sent at the same time a rude and insulting message, to the effect that, "as Lord High Admiral of England, he 'had come to justify the death of that pirate, Sir Andrew Barton, of which James had so often complained, and that he would be in the vanguard of the English army; and as he expected no quarter from his enemies, so would he give none, unless to James himself, should he fall into his hands."

James treated the insulting message of the admiral with silence; but to that of Surrey he replied, "that to meet the English in battle was so much his wish, that had the message of the earl found him at Edinburgh; he should have relinquished all other business to have met him in the field."

James now encamped on Flodden Hill, where it was difficult to attack him, as Hall says there was but one narrow field by which the position could be approached, and at the base of the hill he had placed all his ordnance. On one flank was a marsh, on the other rose the Cheviot Hills.

Many of the Scottish nobles were dissatisfied by the king's ready acceptance of Surrey's challenge. Enough, they said, had been done for honour and to satisfy the claims of France ; and his retreat would compel the English to disperse, as they could not subsist in a district so grievously wasted and plundered already; that a battle must be against increasing odds, and its loss most fatal to the country. They held a council, over which the venerable Lord Lindesay, of the Byres, presided, and laid their views before the king, who became transported with anger, and avowed his determination to fight against the English with his own single hand, if none would follow him. He also vowed that if he was spared to see Scotland, Lord Lindesay should be hanged over his own castle gate. And when the aged Earl of Angus charged La Motte, the French Ambassador, with instigating the rashness of the king, the latter said, "Angus, if you are afraid, go home!"

Then this grand old lord, whose sword had never been in its sheath when Scotland wanted it, burst into tears at an insult so unpardonable.

"If my past life," said he, "does not free me from the suspicion of cowardice, I do not know what can. So long as my body was capable of exertion, I never spared it in defence of my country and king. Now, since age renders me useless in battle, and my counsel is despised, I can but leave my sons and the vassals of Douglas in the field. May Angus's forebodings be unfounded!"

That night he quitted the camp, but his two sons, George, the Master of Angus, and Sir William Douglas, of Glenbervie, with 200 gentleman all of the clan and surname of Douglas, perished to a man in the battle that ensued; while the aged earl, broken-hearted by the calamities of his house and his country, retired to a monastery, and died in the following year.

The Earl of Surrey, with his horse, foot, and cannon, had now advanced to Wooler. The latter are said to have been of inferior make to those of the Scots, but to have been far more numerous and far better served. They were constructed of hoops -and bars, as the first cast-iron guns of English manufacture were made at Buxstead, in Sussex, in 1543, by Ralph Hogge, master founder, who employed as his principal assistant one Peter Baude, a Frenchman. Gun-founding was a French invention, and thus was probably adopted by the Scots earlier than the English.

The adverse hosts were now but four or five miles apart. When the English van came in sight of the Scottish position,

Surrey reconnoitred it, and saw that he could not attack it with hope of success; and having succeeded in his former attempt to pique the romantic honour of the Scottish king, he resolved to try whether he could not lure him from his vantage-ground, and sent to James a herald with a letter reminding him of the accepted gage of battle, and complaining that, instead of remaining in the place where the first messenger had found him, "he had put himself into ground that was more like a fortress than a camp, or any indifferent field where battle might be tried." He therefore invited him to come down from the height and meet him in the open field below - the plain of Milfield - hinting that it was the opinion of the English nobles that any delay of the encounter did not redound to the king's own honour. This missive, which will be found among Ellis's "Original Letters," did not succeed in its object completely.

According to all the laws of war, ancient and modem, the request was utterly unreasonable; and James refused to admit the messenger into his presence. Being now in want of provisions, on the 8th of September, Surrey passed the Till, near Westwood, and, to lure the Scots into action, marched through some rough ground on the east side to Barmoor Wood, two miles from the king's position, and halted for the night. A few cannon-shots were fired by Borthwick at Lord Thomas Howard and a few knights who were seen reconnoitring on an eminence near Ford. Next morning the English resumed their march in a north-westerly direction till near the confluence of the Till and the Tweed, when the vanguard and artillery crossed the former at Twisel Bridge (the beautiful old arch of which still spans the river), while the rear passed at a ford higher up. Having by their detour, with undoubted skill, placed themselves between the King of Scotland and his own country, the English now marched in full array towards Flodden Hill.

On this morning two omens of evil were whispered in the

Scottish ranks. One was that the mysterious man of Linlithgow had been seen in the royal tent at night; and that the field-mice had gnawed the lining of James's helmet.

The Scots seem to have conceived that their position was sufficiently protected on the east side by the deep and sluggish Till, with its perilous fords, and by a battery of guns near the foot of the slope, commanding the bridge of Ford. When the peculiar movement of Surrey was first perceived, James IV imagined naturally that it was the earl's intention to cross the Tweed and ravage Berwickshire, and in this opinion he was confirmed by an Englishman, named Giles Musgrove, who possessed his confidence, and treacherously urged a descent from his position to attack Surrey. Such is the assertion of Buchanan and Ridpath. While the English were crossing the Till, with their van and rear apart, the Scottish leaders entreated the king's permission to attack them; and Borthwick, commander of the artillery, actually fell on his knees', imploring permission to open fire on the bridge with his guns, and thus throw them into confusion. But the king, says Pitscottie, answered Borthwick like a man bereft of judgment, threatening to hang him if he fired a single shot, adding, "I shall have all the enemy in the plain before me, and assay them what they can do."

As soon as he saw the enemy in order of battle, he fired the streets of temporary huts which formed his camp, and marched out to possess the adjacent eminence of Brankston. The Scots came down in five columns, each a bow-shot apart, in perfect silence and order. This absence of sound has been remarked by all historians. "They marched like the Germans, without talking or making any noise," says the gazette of the battle quoted by Pinkerton. Before those columns rolled the white smoke of the burning huts, obscuring the advance of the English, who had crossed the little stream called the Palinsburn, and reached the foot of Brankston Hill, before they perceived the Scots, with all their banners and pennons displayed, at the distance of a quarter of a mile.

The Scots we have said were now only 30,000 strong; the English outnumbered them by 1,000.

The moment Lord Thomas Howard saw the Scots advancing, he dispatched a trooper to his father, with an Agnus Dei which he wore on his breast, as a token, requesting him "to extend his lines with all speed, and to strengthen the van by closing the centre to the left," so as to form the two divisions in one.

Exactly at four in the afternoon of the 9th of September, 1513, this eventful battle began by a cannonade on both sides, for war was modernising now in its forms and appliances. "Then," says an old writer, "out burst the ordnance with fire, flame, and hideous noise, and the master gunner of the English slew the master gunner of Scotland, and beat all his men from their guns, so that the Scottish ordnance did no harm to the Englishmen, but the Englishmen's artillery shot into the midst of the king's battail, and slew many persons, which seeing, the King of Scots and his brave men made the more haste to come to joining."

With their long lances levelled at the charge, the Scottish left wing rushed with such fury on that portion of the English right under Sir Edmund Howard that it was overpowered, disordered, and beaten back, After a desperate resistance, Sir Edmund's banner was taken, he was beaten down, his division routed, and he would have been slain but for timely succour lent him by the bastard Heron, who had joined the English army at the head of a band of wild and reckless outlaws. Sir Edmund, with his routed force, fell back, but Lord Dacre's advance with the reserve of men-at-arms kept Huntley in check; while Home's force, which consisted of undisciplined borderers, left their ranks to plunder over the field.

This enabled Sir Edmund, now reinforced, to attack another division of the Scots led by the Earls of Crawford and Montrose.

Long and resolute was the conflict, but ultimately both these nobles fell, and their men were routed.

On the Scottish right, under Argyle and Lennox, the Macleods, Mackenzies, Macleans, Campbells, and some other Highland clans were severely galled by the archers of Cheshire and Lancashire, led by Sir William Molyneaux and Sir Henry Kickley, till, with a yell of defiance, they rushed forward in wild fury, regardless of the cries and menaces of La Motte, the French Ambassador, and others, who sought to restrain them. With target, claymore, and pole-axe, they flung themselves in a mass upon the enemy. For a moment the shock was tremendous, and the bills and pikes, which had now replaced the bows, reeled and wavered under an onslaught so fierce and unusual. Recovering from the shock, the English columns kept their ranks close, and charging their disorganised assailants in front and flank, routed them, but not without the most dreadful slaughter, amid which the two Scottish earls perished.

While fortune wavered thus upon the wings, the centres, under Surrey and the king, were engaged in a fierce, close, and very dubious conflict. Despite the remonstrances of his courtiers, James, inspired by all the hereditary courage of his race, fought on foot like the rest of his division, exposing his person, so conspicuous by the richness of his arms and armour, wherever strife was thickest, and, surrounded by his faithful and devoted nobles and knights, charged with such fury that the ranks of the English were broken, and Surrey's standard was nearly taken.

It was at this critical moment that the left flank of the Scottish centre was assailed by the columns of Lord Dacre and the Admiral of England, after defeating those of Montrose and Crawford, arid which gave it a terrible shock; but Bothwell came gallantly up with his reserve of spear-men, and made the fight more equal: and new fully 60,000 men, gallant Britons all, were engaged in one close and deadly melee. No quarter was asked on either side, and none was given; and the ground soon became so slippery with blood flowing from the dreadful wounds and gashes inflicted by axes, bills, and two-handed swords, that many of the combatants took off their boots and shoes to ensure a firmer footing.

By this time Sir Edward Stanley, after the total disorder of the Scottish right wing had been achieved, flung himself with all his command on the rear and right flank of the king's division, which was then surrounded on all sides by overwhelming odds. Resolutely did the Scots maintain the conflict; and, flinging themselves in a circle around their beloved king, with the fervour of passionate loyalty and bravery, repelled on every side the attempts to break their dense array.

Well has Scott written of this -

"The English shafts in volleys hailed,
In headlong charge their horse assailed;
Front, flank, and rear, the squadrons sweep,
To break that Scottish circle deep
    Which fought around the king.
But yet, though thick the shafts as snow,
Though charging knights like whirlwinds go,
Though bill-men ply the ghastly blow.
    Unbroken was the ring;
The stubborn spear-men still made good
Their dark, impenetrable wood;
Each stepping where his comrade stood,
    The instant that he fell."

At length King James, mortally wounded in the head by a ball from some unknown hand, and pierced by several arrows, fell dead within a spear's length of Lord Surrey; but his faithful subjects, chiefly knights and nobles, obstinately defended his body, till night and darkness put an end to the carnage.

Surrey was yet uncertain as to the issue of the battle, for the Scottish circle around the dead king was still unbroken, and the division under Lord Home had been victorious. But when day broke on that ghastly scene beside the Till, the Scottish army was found to have quitted the field, leaving seventeen pieces of cannon of various calibre deserted by the side of Flodden Hill.

Solemn thanks for the victory were now offered up on the field, and forty knights created. While this was passing, Lord Home's division and banner appeared hovering near the right flank, and another body of Scots, now supposed to have been a remnant of their centre, appeared in front, as if about to renew the strife, but were dislodged by the English artillery. Among the Scottish guns taken were the "Seven Sisters of Borthwick," who lay dead beside them. According to the official report of the battle, they were "the neatest, the soundest, the best fashioned, the smallest in the touch-hole, and the most beautiful of their size and length that ever were seen."

The loss of the English amounted to about 5,000 men, but few persons of distinction were slain, as the battle was decided chiefly, as usual, by their archers. Sir Brien Tunstall, of Thurland Castle, called, in the romantic language of those days, "Tunstall the Undefiled," either from his white banner or the silver brightness of his armour, as well as from his unstained reputation as a knight, was one of the few Englishmen of rank who fell at Flodden, a battle which spread unparalleled grief and consternation in Scotland.

Of the Scots 10,000 men were slain. With the king perished his natural son, a mere boy, who was Legate-à-latere and Archbishop of St. Andrew's, a student under Erasmus; the Bishops of Caithness and the Isles; Sir William Knowles, Lord High Treasurer and Grand Prior of the Knights of St. John; the

Abbot of Inchaffray, and the Dean of Glasgow; twelve earls, ten lords, and 113 knights, and so many chiefs of families that there was none of eminence in Scotland but had an ancestor slain at Flodden.

Long and fondly did the Scots hope that their king survived, and would yet return to them; many alleging that he was so handsome that he had been spirited away to Fairyland by the Queen of Elphin, or had gone on a pilgrimage to Palestine.

Godwin's Annals record that when James's body was found, it had a deep gash in the neck, and his left hand was nearly hewn off in two places, while many arrow-wounds were on his person. It was recognised by Lord Dacre, was fully identified by the Chancellor of Scotland and others; and was very oddly sent to London, where it was never properly interred, but was lapped in lead, thrown into a lumber-room at Sheen, and ultimately the bones were, in the days of Elizabeth, buried 'among others taken out of the charnel-house of St. Michael's, Wood Street (Stow's "Surrey").

The Battle of Flodden.

The sword and ring of James - perhaps the fatal ring sent by Anne of Bretagne - are still preserved in the Heralds' College, London.

The tomb of Sir William Molyneaux, in Sefton Church, Lancashire, still exists, to record how valiantly he led the archers of Lancashire at Flodden, where he took two banners, and was thanked by a letter from Henry VIII. Save the Selkirk banner, and the pennon of Sir William Keith preserved at Edinburgh, no relics remain of this field in Scotland, except the memory of it.

"No event more immediately calamitous than the defeat at Flodden darkens the Scottish annals," says an eloquent writer. "Shrieks of despair resounded throughout the kingdom. Wives, mothers, and daughters rushed into the streets and highways, tearing their hair, indulging in all the distraction of sorrow; while each invoked some favourite name, a husband, a son, a father, a brother, now blended in one bloody mass of destruction. While the pleasing labours of harvest were abandoned, while an awful silence reigned in the former scenes of rural mirth, the castle and the town echoed to the lamentations of noble matrons and virgins; the churches and chapels were filled with melancholy processions, to deprecate the Divine vengeance, and to chant funeral masses for the slain."

The archers of Ettrick, known in Scotland as the "Flowers of the Forest," perished nearly to a man; and to the present day the sweet, sad, wailing air which is known by that name is almost the invariable Dead March used by all Scottish regiments.

HADDENRIG, 1542 - ANCRUM MOOR, 1545

HADDENRIG

NEARLY THIRTY years elapsed after Flodden before any other great bloodshed ensued upon the borders. But the latter years of the life of Henry VIII, one of the most fickle, self-willed, and absolute of English monarchs, now became occupied by the old story of those days, a war with Scotland and with France.

Several causes contributed to produce a rupture between Henry and his nephew, James V of Scotland.

The latter, satisfied with the faith of his forefathers, declined to engage in theological disputes; and the Pontiff, to rivet him more closely to the apostolical see, bestowed a cardinal's hat upon the most favoured of his counsellors, David Beaton, afterwards Archbishop of St. Andrew's, and sent him a Sword of State, sharpened with much ceremony against England, and now preserved in the castle of Edinburgh. When His Holiness determined to publish the sentence of deprivation against Henry, for his apostacy from Rome, James of Scotland, the Emperor Charles, and Francis of France, promised to join in their endeavours to convert or punish the pervert; and these ended in two conflicts on the borders, and an invasion of the Isle of Wight.

Neither Charles nor Francis, however, showed any activity in enforcing the papal bull; and their idleness induced the King of Scotland to preserve relations of amity with his uncle, Henry. But the latter grew more jealous, both of the religious opinions of James, and of his intimate connection with the French

Court. As if to stigmatise the proceedings of that of England, the Scottish Parliament passed several laws in support of the ancient creed, and of the supremacy of Rome; and in 1542 the usual preliminary forays on the borders began, while twenty-eight Scottish ships were taken at sea.

In the month of August, Sir Robert Bowes, captain of the castle of Norham, and warden of the Eastern Marches, assembled 3,000 horse, for what was then termed a " warden raid," and crossed the frontier into Scotland. He was accompanied on this expedition by his brother, Richard, Sir John Widrington, Sir William Mowbray, and several other knights, together with the exiled Earl of Angus, and his brother, Sir George Douglas, both of whom were banished from Scotland.

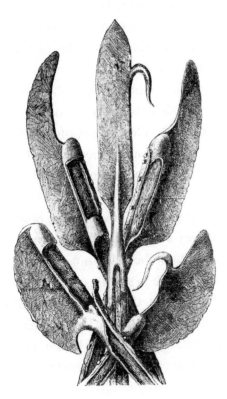

Tuaghs, or Scottish battle-axes, preserved at Edinburgh.

They ravaged all Teviotdale, and were advancing towards Jedburgh, to destroy it with fire and sword, when, a few miles westward of Kelso, their march was stopped at Haddenrig by a force under George Gordon, Earl of Huntley, Knight of St. Michael, to whom James had committed the care of the borders.

The dress and arms of the Scottish borderers were extremely simple. Patten, in his account of Somerset's expedition, observes that, in battle the laird could not be distinguished from the trooper, as all wore the same kind of armour, called a jack, the baron only being distinguished by his sleeves of mail and his head-piece. The borderers in general acted as light cavalry; they rode horses of a small size, but astonishingly active, and trained to move by short bounds through the dangerous morasses that lay along the Scottish frontier. Their offensive weapons were a lance of uncommon length; a sword, either two-handed or of the more modern kind; sometimes a species of battle-axe, called a Jedburgh staff; and, latterly, dags or pistols. Although so much accustomed to move on horseback that they held it degrading to appear otherwise, the Marchmen occasionally acted as infantry, in forming that impenetrable phalanx of spears of which an old English chronicler says that "sooner shall a bare finger, pierce through the skin of an angry hedgehog, than one encounter the brunt of their pikes."

The encounter at Haddenrig was one of border cavalry. With lance and sword they closed in with great fury, and a close and bitter conflict ensued; for there was not a man on either side who had not some private hate to satisfy, or outrage to avenge. Many were speared, shot, unhorsed; and cut down; and so steadily was the contest maintained that victory long remained doubtful; till, at a critical moment, George, Lord Home, came galloping up it the head of 400 lances, and fell upon the flank of Sir Robert Bowes.

This sudden access of force inspirited the Scots, who, after a time, put the English to the rout. The Governor of Norham was taken, together with Sir William Mowbray, Sir John Widrington, Sir George Douglas, and several hundred others. Aware that he might have to die the death of a traitor if captured, the Earl of Angus fought with blind desperation only to escape. A knight had already disarmed and seized him; but Angus closing in, dispatched him with one blow of his dagger, and fled at the full speed of his horse.

Enraged by the loss at Haddenrig, Henry declared war, and ordered the Duke of Norfolk to assemble a numerous army at York. In the same year, James V died of a broken heart, his daughter Mary was born; and more than ever did it seem probable that Henry, by force or marriage, might make Scotland his own.

ANCRUM MOOR

To revenge the rejection of his offers to marry his son, Edward, to Mary Queen of Scots, then in her infancy, he resolved to invade her kingdom. Two knights of approved valour and distinction, Sir Ralph Evers (son of the first and father of the second Lord Ewrie) and Sir Brian Layton, entered Scotland at the head of 3,000 mercenaries, chiefly Germans and Spaniards, 1,500 English borderers, and 700 "assured Scottishmen," chiefly Armstrongs, Turnbulls, and other broken clans; for it would appear that in those lawless times the Scottish borderers were unable to resist the temptation of English gold, and thus not a few of them are mentioned as assisting most infamously in the forays, and as being particularly active in securing plunder. To this they were, probably, the more readily induced by their own hereditary animosities and private quarrels; and nothing more deplorable can be conceived than the state of the border counties, until the total defeat of the English at Ancrum Moor.

On this occasion, Sir Ralph Evers, who was wont to boast that he had "knocked at the gates of Edinburgh," acted with merciless severity; he burned 192 towns, towers, and farm-steadings in the counties of Berwick and Roxburgh; killed 403 men, and took 816 prisoners; seized 10,836 cattle, 12,492 horses, 850 bolls of corn, and other plunder to an amount unknown, according to a return made to his own Government. On the march towards Melrose, he burned the tower of Broomhouse, wherein, says Bishop Lesly, there perished an aged and noble lady, with her whole family.

The Earl of Angus, who had some time before been recalled from exile, and who had large estates in the ravaged districts, was greatly exasperated against the English on account of the losses he had sustained; and also because, in the new spirit of the Reformation, they had some time before defaced the tombs of his ancestors in the abbey of Melrose, for which he swore to write a pardon on their own skins. The Earl of Arran, a weak noble, was at that time Regent of Scotland, during the minority of the infant queen; and the loud complaints of Angus respecting his own losses, and the public disgrace, at length roused him from his timid indolence, and he took the field.

Angus, at the head of 1,000 horse, was following Layton's troops, who, after pillaging Melrose a second time, were moving towards Jedburgh, when a great body of Fifeshire men came up, under Norman Lesly, Master of Rothes - the same wild spirit who afterwards slew Cardinal Beaton, and fell at the battle of St. Quentin. The English were probably unwilling to cross the Teviot while these united forces hung upon their rear, and so they accordingly halted upon the moor of Ancrum. This was on the 12th of February, 1545.

Angus, with a force so small, was painfully undecided as to whether or not he should risk an encounter with such unequal strength, when he obtained fresh succours, in a strong force of borderers, led by Sir Walter Scott, of Buccleuch, who, like Angus, had many wrongs to avenge, particularly on Sir Ralph Evers, who in the preceding year had ravaged all his lands in western Teviotdale, stormed two of his strongest castles, slaughtered some forty of his men, and, as stated in Murdin's State Papers, carried off immense booty.

Buccleuch was a border warrior of great experience, who had evinced high courage at the battle of Melrose; but his military judgment was not turned into rashness by a longing for revenge. His experienced eye saw at once the line of tactics to be followed, and he prevailed upon Angus to draw their combined forces from the eminence they occupied, overlooking the English position, to a piece of level ground called Peniel Haugh, and to send their horses with the camp-boys to another height in the rear.

This stratagem, or movement, was intended to make the English believe that the Scots were taking to flight. Sir Ralph Evers and the other leaders readily fell into the snare; and were eager to pursue, lest the fugitives might escape. The English troops were sorely fatigued by their long march, and by the plunder with which many of them were laden, and were in want of both rest and refreshment; but "advance" was now the order, and they hurried forward, the infantry at a run and the cavalry at a trot, as they fancied, in pursuit.

The trot quickened to a gallop, the men-at-arms believing that all they had to do was to override and cut to pieces a terror-stricken enemy; but, on reaching the summit of the height which the Scots had so craftily abandoned, they were greatly astonished to perceive in the hollow below their serried ranks calmly waiting their approach. Confident of success, from the superiority of their numbers, and from the circumstance that their German and Spanish mercenaries were trained soldiers, who had served in many wars; and believing that these circumstances would make up for their exhaustion and for the disorder into which they had been thrown by the fury of their rush up-hill; the English leaders resolved on an attack, and continued to advance.

At that moment a heron, disturbed by the tumult of sounds, flew up from some adjacent sedges; and the Earl of Angus, in a spirit of elation and confidence, exclaimed, laughingly, "Oh, that I had here my white goss-hawk; for then we should all yoke (join) at once!"

Under Sir George Bowes and Sir Bryan Layton, the cavalry, of which their forces were chiefly composed, charged briskly, but were repelled by the Scottish spear-men, who now began to advance, and hurled them back in confusion on the main body, when many men were trod down by their comrades' horses. This thrust the second line back upon the third. Discharges of arquebuses were exchanged on both sides; but as the smoke of these was blown by the wind among the English, who had also the oblique rays of the evening sun shining in their eyes, neither leaders nor banners could be distinguished. Charging forward, horse and foot, the Scots fiercely drove the broken ranks against each other. They were thus impeded, and unable to use their weapons effectively, or plant in the turf those long rests over which the arquebuses were fired; and as each man of the wavering force began to seek an escape for himself from this sudden scene of helpless and fatal disorder, a rout became inevitable.

Suddenly amid them there was a cry of "Remember Broomhouse!" and then the 700 "assured Scots," the Armstrongs, Turnbulls, and Halls, with this shout, tore off their red St. George's Crosses, and, making common cause with their already victorious countrymen, turned with axe and spear, in unsparing severity, upon the now broken and flying enemy. The peasantry of the neighbourhood, hitherto only spectators of the brief conflict, now drew near to intercept and cut down the English, who were easily distinguishable by the red cross on their white surcoats; and even women, whose hearts had been steeled by their barbarities, joined in the pursuit, and shrieked to the conquerors to "Remember Broomhouse!"

One of these, still remembered as "the maiden Lilliard," mingled in the fray when she saw her lover fall; and her gravestone, lately renewed, still lies near the field.

The battle became, as usual then, a pitiless slaughter, which lasted till nightfall. Of the enemy there fell 800 men, among whom were Sir Ralph Evers and Sir Brian Layton, to the intense satisfaction of the Earl of Angus; while 1,000 were made prisoners, among whom were many men of rank, whose ransoms proved valuable. One was an alderman of London, named Read, who, having contumaciously refused to pay his portion of a sum demanded from that city by Henry, was sent by him to serve on foot against the Scots, whom, says Ridpath,

The Battle of Ancrum Moor.

he found more exorbitant in their exactions than the tyrannical Tudor.

The Scots loss was very trifling. They lost no time in following up their victory. The whole camp equipage of the English was found in Melrose, and the border districts were everywhere cleared of them. The Regent embraced the victor, Angus, and carried him off to Stirling to receive the congratulations of the Queen Dowager, Mary of Lorraine; and a proclamation was issued that all who had adopted the red cross should be pardoned on returning to their allegiance.

The two English knights were honourably interred, in Melrose Abbey. The coffin of Evers, an entire stone, was found there in 1813, a little to the left of the great altar. His skeleton was then entire, but speedily crumbled into dust.

Shortly after this victory at Ancrum Moor, and the expulsion of the English from the border counties, word was sent to the Scottish Court that Francis I was about to prove himself a formidable enemy to England on her own soil, and the faithful ally of Scotland, by invading the former, and carrying out a project he had in view; and this was nothing less than capture of the Isle of-Wight, which he conceived might be fortified, and maintained as a possession of France.

- C H A P T E R   I I I -
ISLE OF WIGHT, 1545

IN CONFORMITY with his promises, Francis I, began to make preparations, not only for expelling the English garrisons from Boulogne, Calais, and other places, but to invade their country in return.

With this view, he equipped in several of the ports of France one hundred and fifty great ships, and sixty of smaller tonnage, with ten more carracks hired from the Genoese. He sent orders to Captain Paulin to bring five-and-twenty row galleys from the Levant (in imitation of Louis XII, who had four from the same place), and to anchor them at the mouth of the Seine; where a catastrophe occurred. Francis gave a magnificent dinner to the ladies of his Court on board the greatest vessel - one armed with a hundred pieces of cannon, and which De Mezeray describes as " the most stately vessel belonging to the sea" - but the cooks by their carelessness set it on fire; her guns went off in succession, and, singularly enough, seem to have been shotted in harbour, and so did infinite mischief to all the craft around her. At last she blew up - a circumstance "which," we are told, "greatly disordered the feast, and gave an ill presage of that expedition." In this fleet Père Daniel states, the French had one ship carrying 100 guns entirely of brass.

Francis mustered an army of 40,000 men; to these he intended to add 12,000 German Free Lances, to block up Boulogne by land, as well as by sea, so that it should be impossible for the English to relieve it. To execute this project he sent a reinforcement to the marshal commanding, Odoard Seigneur du Biez et de Vendôme, ordering him to finish a fort that had been begun at Portet; and then coming to Hâvre de Grâce in the middle of August, he ordered the fleet to sail for England.

On the other hand, Henry VIII was not idle. To expedite by his presence the naval operations that were being carried on at Portsmouth for the prosecution of the war, he took up his residence there. Burnet states that the ships on both sides in this war were merely hired merchantmen; but only some could have been such, for the purposes of transport.

On the 18th of July the French fleet, stated to be 200 sail, under Claude d'Annebaut, Baron de Retz, created Admiral of France in 1543, was reported to be off St. Helen's, and menacing the Isle of Wight, after having landed some detachments at Brighton, then the fishing village of Brighthelmstone, to burn and spoil the country. But the beacon-fires were soon set ablaze on the green downs of Sussex; and Holinshed tells us that these detachments were beaten off to their own ships, with considerable loss.

Henry at their approach ordered all the ships that were ready - not more than a hundred according to one account; only sixty sail according to another - to get under weigh, and meet them. The fleet was commanded by Sir John Dudley, Baron of Lisle, Admiral of England in 1543. On their departure from Portsmouth Harbour, the English, like the French, had a catastrophe. The *Mary Rose*, one of the largest ships in the navy, carrying sixty guns, was overset by a sudden squall of wind; her lower deck ports being open, and within only sixteen inches of the water. Thus she filled and went down instantly; and her commander, Sir George Carew, and every man on board perished. A footnote to Schomberg's "Naval Chronology" states that "some authors inform us that she was sunk in the action, and that the *Great Harry* nearly shared the same fate, but was towed into the harbour." King Henry had dined on board the *Mary Rose* that day, and had only returned to the shore a few hours before the accident. In the year 1835 some curious relics of this old ship were fished up; several guns of hoops and rings, the stone shot then in use, with portions of her timbers, being among the articles found. Schomberg ("Naval Chronology") states that the first mention of iron balls for cannon is distinctly made in 1550, when Boulogne was restored to France.

It may be mentioned here, that it was in Henry's reign that the Royal Navy first became a distinct profession. The king fixed salaries to admirals, vice-admirals, captains, and seamen; and since then we have had a constant succession of officers in the service.

Though greatly inferior in number, Dudley's fleet met that of D'Annebaut; but a very indecisive action ensued, as the French did not seem to care much for coming to close quarters. The brunt of the action was borne by the *Great Harry*; and there were many sharp engagements between the galleys, of Captain Paulin and some of the smaller vessels of the English, which M. du Bellay, a French writer, calls "*rambarges*," but which we name "pinnaces." These were light, long, and narrow craft, for sails and oars; and, being easily handled, were very effective in attacking the galleys, which they put to the rout.

The skirmishing - for it was not a close engagement - continued for two days, with cannon, hackbut, and bow, but the damage on both sides was very trifling. The English fleet retired beyond or within the sands, seeking to lure the larger French vessels after them. Admiral d'Annebaut, on consulting his pilots as to how they might be attacked, was told by them "that it was impossible, because the channel which led to the place where they lay was so narrow that scarcely four ships could sail abreast" (no very sufficient reason), "and that, besides, there was no venturing among those sands without pilots who knew them."

Finding that the galleys failed to lure the larger ships out, and that they were beaten off by the smaller; on the land breeze rising, D'Annebaut closed in towards the Isle of Wight, and landed 2,000 troops in three different places, and several villages were burned and destroyed.

One of the officers, Pietro Strozzi, a noble cavalier, banished from Italy in consequence of some quarrel with the House of Medici, and who subsequently served against the English in Scotland, and died a Marshal of France and Lord of Epernay, landed near a little fort, the guns of which had annoyed the galleys. On the approach of his force, it was precipitately abandoned; but his people killed a few of the retreating garrison, and burned all the houses about it.

Another division, led by the Sieur de Tais, who was general of the infantry, and by the Baron de la Garde, landed without opposition; but had not penetrated far into the isle before the inhabitants gathered in arms, and made some head against them, taking possession of ground where they could attack the invaders with advantage, and where, when they chose to retire, they were safe from pursuit, unless the enemy followed in disorder, and exposed themselves to further loss. The Sieur de Tais, therefore, had to fall back.

The Captains Marsay and Pierrebon, who led the third, were both wounded; and their party found it necessary to retreat to their boats, and pull off with all speed to the ships. Meantime, the other troops who had been left on board, incited by the flames of those villages which Strozzi had fired, and seeing no one on the adjacent shore, landed without leave, to enjoy a little pillage; but getting among some hilly ground were attacked by both horse and foot, and driven down to the beach. There they rallied, under protection of a fire from the ships; and, being reinforced, again advanced against the islanders, who in turn retreated, and broke down a bridge to prevent further pursuit (Southey's "Naval History").

The admiral now held council how to proceed. In this assembly it was proposed by one "to force a passage into

Attack on the Isle of Wight.

Portsmouth Harbour, and destroy the English fleet which still lay there." But the hazard of this enterprise was too great; and the captains urged that by securing the Isle of Wight, in the name of the King of France it would eventually give them possession of Portsmouth. They could always be sure of a passage from the island either to Spain or Flanders; and the land itself could be cultivated, so as to feed any garrison they might think proper to leave there.

"These," says Southey, quoting Du Bellay, "were great utilities, and worthy of profound consideration; but, on the other hand, the difficulties that occurred were not less considerable. The Sieurs de Tais and de Saint Remy, and others who were versed in such matters, agreed in opinion that it would be necessary to erect their fortress at the same time, on the plans which had been deemed best suited to that purpose. The ground was semicircular in its form, and at the points of the semicircle two forts were required to defend the road and protect their own fleet; a third was necessary for lodging the troops. The cost of these works would be excessive, It would not be possible to complete them in less than three months, even if 6,000 pioneers were employed; and the place being, as it were, in the heart of the enemy, less than 6,000 soldiers ought not to be left there, but it was impossible to leave so many now, and retain enough for manning the ships. Nor were these the only objections. The fleet could not depart till the works should be in a defensible state; but it was impossible for them to stay there so long, because they had no port to secure them from the winds, neither were they victualled for such a time. The rainy and stormy season was coming on, when the ships would be in danger; and the soldiers on shore would be exposed to the effects of the weather, without tents or covering of any kind. These arguments had such weight that even those who were for taking possession of the isle submitted to them, and agreed that the intention must be deferred till the king's further pleasure could be known."

"For my part," says Martin du Bellay, "without offence to the Sieurs de Tais and de Saint Remy, it appears to me that, considering the desire the king had to secure himself against his enemy, the King of England, and the means which he then possessed, an opportunity for so doing was at that time presented which will neither easily nor soon be found again."

Admiral d'Annebaut now sailed towards Dover, and made occasional landings for the purpose of pillage; but so resolute and active was the resistance of the people, that the French suffered more loss than they inflicted.

Meanwhile, Dudley, who had been reinforced at Portsmouth, joyfully received the king's orders once more to put forth to sea and attack the enemy. His own orders to his captains were, that when a convenient time came for engaging, "our van-ward shall make with their vanward, if they have any; and if they be in one company, our vanward, taking the advantage of the wind, shall set upon the foremost rank, bringing them out of order, and our vice-admiral shall seek to board their vice-admiral; and every captain shall choose his equal as near as he may."

"The last part of this order," says Creasy, in his "Invasions of England," "reminds us of one of Nelson's before going into action at Trafalgar - 'No captain can do wrong who lays his ship alongside one of the enemy.'"

Sir John Dudley overtook the fleet of D'Annebaut between Brighton and Shoreham, and some manoeuvring ensued to gain the advantage of the wind. There were light airs and a nearly calm sea, which contributed greatly to the advantage of the French, who had so many row-galleys, and were independent of the wind.

On the 15th of August some distant cannonading took place between the fleets; but next morning, when the wind had freshened, and given Dudley some hope of assailing them with advantage, he saw them in full retreat, as he expresses it, "sailing into the seawards." The previous day's encounter was called the battle of Brighton, or Brighthelmstone.

For the injuries done at the Isle of Wight, Dudley retaliated by crossing the Channel and sacking the town of Treport, on the coast of France; and thus the operations which had begun so ominously were concluded honourably for England.

- C H A P T E R   I V -
PINKIE, 1547

THE YEAR 1547 found England and Scotland again at war. In that year Henry VIII died, leaving behind him a reputation very different from that which his earlier years presaged. He divorced his first wife upon the convenient plea of conscience, that he might marry one handsomer and younger. He murdered the second through satiety, and a growing passion for another. He married a third twenty-four hours after the execution of the second, who, happily for herself, died in a few months. He divorced the fourth, because she was less beautiful than her portrait. The fifth he beheaded, on very questionable evidence; and the sixth he would have burned at Smithfield as a heretic. And yet, by his will, "he earnestly begs the blessed Virgin Mary, the mother of Jesus Christ, and the whole company of heaven, to pray to God continually for him" ("Acta Regis," Vol. III).

It was also enjoined by Henry's will that a marriage should take place, if possible, between Edward VI and the young Queen Mary of Scotland, then in her fourth year. But the Scottish people were all, save a few nobles in English pay, averse to such a measure; so the Protector Somerset soon evinced, by one of the very first acts of his Government, that he was resolved to carry Henry's dying wishes into effect. He determined to lead an army into the northern kingdom; and addressed a letter to all the principal nobility, reminding them of the league by which they had bound themselves to assist the deceased King of England in the accomplishment of his designs.

These measures were very unwise, and only calculated to increase the rancour of the Scots, and bind them faster to France.

The Earl of Arran, who was then Regent of Scotland,

though a man naturally indolent, and of unsettled principles, exerted himself to create a vigorous union against the English. He became active in his military preparations; he laboured to strengthen the defences of the borders, and to have the people trained by wapinschaws to arms. He encouraged the equipment of privateers, as the only substitute for the national fleet which Dudley had destroyed in the last war; and he anxiously strove to soothe those sanguinary feuds, by which the chiefs and barons wasted the strength of the country, and when there was peace abroad, involved it in all the horrors of war at home. In the summer of 1547 he established a line of beacons upon the hills near and along the coast of the German Ocean and the Firth of Forth, from St. Abb's Head to Linlithgow. Mounted sentinels were stationed to convey intelligence of any hostile appearance; and all persons were strictly forbidden to leave their residences or remove their goods, as it was resolved to defend Scotland at every hazard of life and blood.

It was of this new and wanton war that the Earl of Huntly remarked in the Scottish Parliament that he "disliked not the match, but he hated the manner of wooing."

Several acts of hostility preluded the battle to come. Hayward mentions that a small ship, called the *Pansy*, attacked at sea "the *Lion*, a principal ship of Scotland. The fight began afar off and slow, but when they approached it grew furious; but the *Pansy* so applied her shot that the *Lion's* oar-loop (deck) was broken, her sails and tackling torn, and, lastly, she was boarded and taken," but perished off Harwich, with all that were in her.

Edward, Duke of Somerset, Protector of England during the minority of Edward VI, arrived at Newcastle on the 27th of August, at the head of 14,000 Englishmen, and many bands of foreign auxiliaries, trained and reckless soldiers, whose trade was war and rapine. He had with him 15 pieces of cannon, and 900 wagons laden with stores. Sir Francis Fleming was Master of the Ordnance, and had with him 1,500 pioneers, under Captain John Brem, to clear the way, for the Scottish roads were then rough and steep. Master William Patten, who accompanied this army as Judge-Marshal, has left us a minute account of the campaign, and an accurate list of all the commanders in the Protector's army; to aid which were thirty ships of war, under Edward, Lord Clinton and Say, K.G. (afterwards High Admiral of England), and thirty-two transports, under Sir William Wodehouse, vice-admiral, came to anchor at the mouth of the Tyne.

Patten's work, which is extremely scarce, is entitled "The Expedition into Scotland of the Most Worthy Fortunate Prince, Edward, Duke of Somerset, &c., made in the First Yere of his Maistie's Most Prosperous Reign, and set out by way of Diarie by W. Patten, London. Vivat Victor! Out of the Parsonage of St. Mary Hill, in London, this xxviii of January, 1548."

Lord Grey of Wilton, Lieutenant of Boulogne, was High-Marshal and Captain-General of the Horse, who were all cap-à-pie, in full but light armour. Sir Ralph Vane commanded the men-at-arms and demi-lances, who were 4,000 strong. Sir Francis Bryan (in the following year Governor of Ireland) was captain of the light horse, 2,000 strong; Sir Thomas Darcy led King Edward VI's band of Gentlemen Pensioners.

Sir Peter Mewtas was commander of the German infantry, who were all clad in buff coats, pot helmets, and gorgets, and were armed with arquebuse and sword.

Don Pedro de Gamboa led the mounted Spanish arquebusiers. These trained foreigners, who were accustomed to discipline, and had served in many wars, were the flower of Somerset's army. Many of them were veterans who had served at the siege of Rhey, in 1521, when fire-arms were first used by the Spaniards. Edward Shelly led the men-at-arms of Boulogne, who, like the mercenaries, were well trained, but were Englishmen, who had

41

been long in garrison there, and were clad in blue doublets, slashed and faced with red, and some were entirely in the latter colour. Sir Ralph Sadler, the famous diplomatist, was the treasurer, and Sir James Wilford was provost-marshal of this army, which was in every way the best ordered that had ever entered Scotland.

Scotland was at this time full of traitors; for there was found in the July of that year, in St. Andrew's, a register-book, containing the names of 200 Scottish nobles and barons who had secretly bound themselves to promote the designs of England. "The most prominent among these most infamous traitors," says a recent "History of Scotland," "were the Earls of Bothwell, Cassillis, and Marischal, Lord Kilmaurs, eldest son of the Earl of Glencairn, Lord Grey, and the notorious Sir George Douglas. Bothwell had promised to transfer his allegiance to the English Government, and to surrender to them his strong castle of Hermitage, on condition that he should receive the hand of the Duchess of Suffolk, aunt to the young English monarch. The Earls of Athol, Crawford, Enrol, and Sutherland had been tampered with, and intimated their willingness to join the English faction, provided they were honestly entertained. Glencairn - a veteran in treachery and statecraft - had secretly made overtures to the Protector, offering to co-operate in the invasion of Scotland, with 2,000 of his vassals ; assuring Somerset that, if furnished with money, he would hold the Regent in check till the arrival of the invading army." And it was under the auspices of titled miscreants such as these that the Scottish Commons, ever most loyal and true to their country, now prepared to defend her.

Somerset entered Scotland on the 2nd of September, and marched along the shore of the German Sea, keeping in view of his fleet of sixty-four sail, which bore towards the Firth of Forth. Without opposition he reached a place called the Peaths, a tremendous ravine, now crossed by a bridge, perhaps the greatest of its kind in Europe, as it is 300 feet in length and 240 feet in height. "Abrupt, precipitous, and narrow, this ravine formed one of the great passes into Scotland; and, being of easy defence, was deemed a kind of sluice, by which the tide of war would be loosened or confined at pleasure." But now the Regent, Arran, had taken no measures to defend it.

For a whole day Captain Brem, with his pioneers, and Sir Francis Fleming, with his gunners, toiled, "with much puffyng and payne," says Patten, to drag the cannon and carriages through that savage ravine; while the Protector sent detachments against various feudal fortresses in the vicinity, which were stormed and blown up by gunpowder. Among them were Lord Home's castles of Dunglassand Thornton; and Inverwick, a tower of the Hamiltons. Before the explosion of the mines, "it would have rued any good housewife's heart," says Patten, "to have beholden the great slaughter our men made of the brood geese and good-laying hennes which the wives had penned up in the holes and cellars of the castle. The spoil was not rich, to be sure; but of white bread, oaten cakes, and Scottish ale was indifferent good store, and soon bestowed among my lord's soldiers accordingly.

The Earl of Warwick led the vanguard; Somerset the main body; and Thomas, Lord Dacres, of Gillesland, the rear. Each of these three great columns was flanked in its march by horse, and each had artillery, with pioneers to guard and clear the way before them.

Through Haddingtonshire the duke pushed onward to the Tyne, which his army crossed by the same old bridge that spans it still; but not unopposed, as the peasantry and vassals of the house of Hepburn, who had no share in their master's treason, opened a fire of falcons and calivers from his castle of Hailes, while a brisk attack was made upon the defiling columns by Dandy Kerr, a famous border marauder, whose troopers, being lightly armed, were driven off by the English cavalry, under Lord Warwick. Laying all the fertile country in flames, they continued their march, till they halted on the 7th at Long Niddry, where the coast is flat and low, and where Somerset could communicate with his fleet, which had then come to anchor in Leith Roads.

He was now aware that a Scottish army was concentrated somewhere in his neighbourhood, as parties of light horse were seen galloping along the eminences, hallooing, and brandishing their spears, as if in defiance. Nevertheless, Lord Clinton was courageous enough to come on shore and attend a Council of War, at which it was arranged that he should moor the fleet near the mouth of the Esk, to co-operate with the land forces, which Somerset proposed to halt finally on the green links or downs eastward of the town of Musselburgh; where on the evening of the 8th he saw the camp of the Scottish army, consisting of 36,000 men, mustered by the Fiery Cross, covering all the long green slope known as Edmondstone Edge, at the base of which the Esk flows into the firth.

Somerset pitched his tent near the village of Saltpreston, and the whole country around it was laid desolate by fire; all who failed to escape perished by the sword, and for three entire days the whole landscape was shrouded in the smoke of blazing hamlets, farms, mills, and stackyards. All this was visible from the camp of the exasperated Scots, whose white tents, in four long rows or streets lay from east to west along Edmondstone Edge. These were surmounted in many instances by the banners of nobles, chiefs, and towns; and amid these tents the armour and weapons of so many men caused a glitter that seemed incessant to the eyes of the English.

As in many other battles which the Scots lost by the treason of their nobles or the imbecility of their leaders, rather than any other cause, the first position of the Earl of Arran was a strong one. The Esk, deeper, broader, and more rapid then than now, lay in front; its banks were steep, rocky, and covered with wood; the only avenue to the position was the old Roman bridge which still spans the stream, and this Arran had barricaded, planted with cannon, and manned with archers. The left flank, towards the sea, was protected by an intrenchment of turf, mounted with cannon; while a deep and dangerous morass effectually covered the right. Such was the position of the Scots before the sanguinary battle of Pinkey, or Musselburgh, as the English named it. It barred the way to Edinburgh, where the queen-dowager, the mother of the little Queen Mary, anxiously awaited the result. To have assailed it would have been, perhaps, a hopeless task; and Somerset began to fear that he might yet have to retreat.

As the evening closed the Scots could see the English fleet coming to anchor by stem and stern, with their broadsides towards the shore.

Next morning 1,500 Scottish light cavalry, mosstroopers, under George, Lord Home, rode along the slope of Fawside Hill, in sight of Somerset's camp. Their horses were strong and hardy; and they galloped to and fro, whooping, and taunting the English by injurious epithets to attack them. At last they ventured so close to the camp that Lord Grey of Wilton obtained permission to try the effect of his men-at-arms upon them. At the head of 1,000 of these, with the demi-lances of Sir Ralph Vane, on barbed steeds, he came forth to the attack; and both bodies of cavalry engaged with a ringing cheer that was heard in each of the camps. They met with lances in the rest, and hundreds were killed and wounded on both sides.

It was impossible for the Scottish troopers, whose horses, were, as Patten says, "naked," i.e., without armour, to stand against cavalry who were completely mailed, both horse and man; they were soon broken, but, though losing all order, they continued the conflict along the whole slope of Fawside Hill. Lord Home was unhorsed, and so severely wounded that he died afterwards of the stab at Edinburgh; his son, the Master of Home, was struck from his horse, and, together with the Laird of Garscadden and Captain Crawford, of Jordanhill, taken prisoner by the Earl of Warwick.

This affair, the prelude to the bloodier drama of the morrow, filled the Scots with greater wrath; and the English, though aware that they must either win a battle or be destroyed, with emotions of triumph which they cared not to conceal, for all night long their camp rang with sounds of merriment and acclamation.

Somerset perceived that the Scottish camp was commanded by the hill of Inveresk, and by the higher parts of the lane that led to the opposite hill of Fawside; and these places he meant to occupy by cannon, after a reconnaissance about dusk. As he rode back to camp, "he was overtaken," says Tytler, "by a Scottish herald, with his glittering tabard on, accompanied by a trumpeter, who brought a message from Arran, the governor. The herald said his first errand was for an exchange of prisoners;

Lord Grey of Wilton's charge at Pinkie.

his second to declare that his master, eager to avoid the effusion of Christian blood, was willing to allow him to retreat on honourable conditions. The trumpeter next addressed the duke, informing him that, in case such terms were not accepted, his master, the Earl of Huntly, willing to bring the quarrel to a speedy conclusion, was ready to encounter him with twenty to twenty, ten to ten, or, if he would so far honour him, man to man. To these messages Somerset made a brief and temperate reply. "As for thy master," said he, addressing the trumpeter, "he lacketh some discretion to send his challenge to one who, by reason of the weighty charge he bears - no less than the government of the king's person and the protection of his realm - hath no power to accept it, whilst there are yet many noble gentlemen here, his equals in rank, to whom he might have addressed his cartel without fear of refusal." At this moment the Earl of Warwick broke eagerly in, telling the messenger that he would not only accept the challenge, but would give him a hundred crowns if he brought back his master's consent. "Nay," observed Somerset, "the Earl of Huntly is not equal to your lordship; but, herald, tell the governor, and the Earl of Huntly also, that we have now spent some time in your country, our force is but a small company - yours far exceeds us - yet bring me word they will meet us in a plain field, and thou shalt have a thousand crowns for thy pains, and thy masters fighting enough."

So confident were the Scots of victory, that during the night many of the leaders amused themselves with playing at dice for the disposal and ransoms of the prisoners.

In reality, Somerset was anxious to come to some arrangement. He had wasted the country so much that food had become scarce, and it was lucky for him that the Scots were ignorant of this circumstance. That night, to make a final effort to avert hostilities, he addressed a letter to Arran, in which he declared his readiness to retreat out of the kingdom on the single condition that the Scots would keep their young queen in their own country until she had reached a marriageable age, and could decide for herself; but this proposal was rejected with disdain.

By the dawn of next day, the 10th of September, 1547 - a clear and beautiful one - the English army was observed to be in motion. Somerset had sent some of his artillery to the green summit of Inveresk on one flank, and to Crookston Loan on the other, from whence they could open a fire upon the camp of the Scots, towards whom his whole force began to advance in three great columns - Warwick still leading the first, the duke himself the second, and Dacres the third - but on coming into the fertile plain, which was pleasantly diversified by clumps of trees, and through which a little stream called the Pinkey flows, great was the joy and astonishment of the English to find that the Scots had left their strong position, to meet in the open field his well-trained mercenaries and better-appointed army.

Most rashly and unwisely, the Regent of Scotland had mistaken the first movements of the enemy for an intention to seek safety in flight, by a precipitate rush over the sands of Musselburgh towards their ships; and his sole alarm was lest, after an invasion so uncalled for, and devastations so merciless, they should escape unpunished. Thus he had resolved at once to cross the Esk, to get between them and the sea; and this movement he executed in defiance of the advice of his most skilful soldiers, and with an army whose chief weapons were those of the Middle Ages, while the English had many of the more modern appliances for war, particularly those in the hands of the Germans, Spaniards, and the men of Boulogne and Calais, who had arquebuses, hand-guns, and pistols.

As the Scots, after defiling over the Roman bridge, began to form upon the plain, the English cannon, armed now with iron shot, made many a ghastly lane in their ranks, causing their banners to sway, and their tall ash spears, which an old writer has likened unto a field of ripe corn, to wave to and fro, as if beneath the breath of the wind.

The centre was led by the Regent, and consisted of the clans from Strathearn, with the men of the Lothians, Kinross, and Stirlingshire, who were the flower of the Scottish infantry. There, under their own banner, and led by the provost, marched 800 chosen men of Edinburgh. This division was 18,000 strong. The right wing was composed of 6,000 Western Highlanders and men of the Isles, under Argyle and the chiefs of Macleod and Macgregor. On its flanks and rear were artillery.

The left wing consisted of 10,000 infantry of the eastern counties, led by Archibald, Earl of Angus, flanked by cannon and light horse; and with it marched a singular battalion, consisting of more than 1,000 Scottish monks, drawn forth, to battle in fear of the English Reformation spreading into Scotland more than it had done. Save their armour, which was generally black, they wore white, grey, or red surcoats, with crosses, to distinguish them as Black, Grey, or Red Friars; and they carried with them a standard of white silk, which had been solemnly consecrated by the Abbot of Dunfermline. Thereon was depicted a woman on her knees before a cross, and over her head was the legend, "Afflictæ Ecclesiæ ne obliviscaris."

Patten describes the Lowland infantry as being clad all "alyke in jackes covered with white leather, doublets of the same or white fustian, and most commonly all whits hosen." Why white is somewhat singular.

The Scottish spears were eighteen feet long; and thus when the infantry, in the old fashion of their country, were formed in squares, the first rank knelt, the second sloped, the third stood erect; but all three with their weapons pointed at three angles towards the foe.

On this day the royal standard of England was borne by Sir

Andrew Flammock, a knight of proved valour; that of Scotland was borne by Findlay Mhor Farquharson, of Invercauld, who was killed.

After passing the church of Inveresk, the left flank of the Scots was severely galled by the fire from the English ships. The Master of Graham and twenty-five gentlemen fell, and the Highland archers, under Argyle, were thrown into confusion. This made the Scottish lines -move to the right, with the object of gaining the slope of Fawside Hill, that from thence they might attack the enemy. But the latter, being more skilfully led, had anticipated that movement by planting their artillery there in such a manner that they could fire over the heads of their own men full upon the Scots, whose right wing came up the slope at such a pace that, says Patten, they seemed " rather horsemen than footmen."

As soon as Somerset perceived this movement of the Scots, he ordered Lord Grey to attack their right wing with the cavalry and the mounted Spanish arquebusiers, and keep them in check

Inveresk.

till his other divisions were in position on the slope of the hill. The wing halted in the midst of a ploughed field, the squares bristling with spears in the triple order described. Galloping over the soft and heavy ground, the mailed men-at-arms charged the Scottish spearmen again and again in vain, and many were unhorsed and slain by the furious thrusts of the long weapons, while the Scots, according to Patten, taunted them as " loons, tykes (i.e., dogs), and heretics."

"Herewith," he continues, "waxed it very hot on both sides, with pitiful cries, horrible roar and thundering of guns; besides, the sky darkened above-head with the smoke of shot; the sight of the enemy in front, the danger of death on every side, the bullets and arrows flying everywhere so thick, it was death to fly and danger to fight. The whole face of the field was to the eye and ear so heavy, so deadly lamentable, and terribly confused."

Grey and his cavalry could make no impression whatever on those solid squares of Scottish infantry, while 200 of his men were slain, and among them was Edward Shelly, " Lieutenant of the Bulleners," Ratcliff, Preston, Clarence, and other veteran English officers, who were dispatched by "the whinger," which the Scots carried in their belts. Here Lord Edward Seymour, son of the Duke of Somerset, had his horse killed under him, and Sir Andrew Flammock nearly lost the royal standard. He saved the silk, but the staff was torn out of his hands. Lord Grey was severely wounded in the mouth and neck; and, according to Hayward, had some Scottish cavalry come up at that moment, Somerset had lost the day, for the English men-at-arms were utterly defeated.

The present farmhouse called Barbauchly marks the scene of this encounter.

Unable to pursue Lord Grey, the Scottish left, under Angus, halted, unwilling to advance against the main body of the enemy till certain of support. At that crisis, the Earl of Warwick galloped through the ranks of Grey, disengaged the men-at-arms from the infantry, among whom they had been mingling, and, with the assistance of Sir Ralph Sadler, led forward the Spanish squadrons of Don Pedro Gamboa. These arquebusiers were clad in complete mail; and galloping close up to the squares, they fired their volleys straight into the faces of the Scottish spearmen. The German foot hackbutiers, under Sir Peter Mewtas, now came to the front to second this attack, and then the English archers with their shafts, while the cannon from the hill were firing on the right flank. Under this quadruple discharge, against which they had nothing to oppose but their spears, the division of Angus fell back,, but in good order, upon the main body, under the Earl of Arran. Many of the Highlanders, who were dispersed over the field, already plundering, after their usual custom, mistook this necessary rearward movement for a full retreat, and began to fly in all directions.

The wretched panic speedily spread to the centre, which was chiefly composed of the burgh troops; and though they were still

The fight for the standard at Pinkie.

a quarter of a mile distant from the enemy, and had never been engaged, they threw down their weapons, and fled in confusion.

"They fly! they fly!" was the shout of the English.

The Scottish left, or vanguard, under Angus, might still have withstood the advance of Warwick had they been supported, but now they would not sacrifice themselves. Those squares which had so lately shown an impenetrable a front to the foe were observed first to undulate to and fro "like a steely sea agitated by the wind; after a few moments, breaking into a thousand fragments, they dispersed in all directions."

All was lost now; the ground over which the flight and pursuit lay was as thickly strewed with spears as a floor with rushes. Helmets, bucklers, swords, daggers, wheel-lock pistols, banners, and fragments of armour cast away by their owners as impediments to speed, covered all the fields and meadows; while the English men-at-arms and demi-lances, exasperated by their late defeat and by seeing some of their dead stripped and mangled by the Highlanders, pursued the fugitives at full speed, slaying them thick and fast with sword and lance, crying to each other the while, "Remember Panierhaugh!" referring to the battle of Ancrum.

They spared none but those from whom a heavy ransom was expected.

The fugitives fled three several ways. One mighty mass took the way to Leith by the sands; another made direct for Edinburgh by the Figget Moor and Holyrood Park; while by far the most numerous body turned towards Dalkeith, in the hope that the morass which protected the right of their camp might prove a saving obstacle.

The autumnal wind bore the noise of the battle at times to Edinburgh; but when the English infantry reached Edmondstone Edge, and found themselves amid the plunder of the Scottish camp equipage, the exulting shout they raised could be distinctly heard in the streets of the city, where that day's slaughter made 360 widows.

The Scots by thousands threw themselves into the Esk, a deep river then, and perished miserably under the fire of the cannon from the ships, the fire of the Spaniards and Germans, or by the swords of the English when they scrambled to the bank. On the narrow Roman bridge the press of the living and choke of the dead and dying, men and horses, were frightful; for Lord Clinton's great ship lay broadside on at the river's mouth (a proof of how much the water has shallowed) pointing her cannon on the flying masses; and there were slain the Lord Fleming, the Masters of Buchan, Livingstone, Ogilvy, and Erskine, all the sons of earls; the Lairds of Lochinvar, Merchiston, Craigcrook, Priestfield, Lee, and others, till the barricade of mail-clad dead impeded all further passage. Of the battalion of monks, all nearly perished to a man, and their holy banner was found upon the field. The Esk was literally crimsoned with blood, for the mass of the slain perished on its banks, "the English having vowed that if victorious they should kill many and spare few."

The castle of Fawside, near the field, was set on fire by them; the windows were all grated, and as none within it were suffered to come forth, "for their good will all were burned or smothered within" (Patten). He elsewhere admits that the aspect of the field was terrible - so thick were the corpses; "some without legs, some houghed and half dead, many with their heads cloven, the brains of sundry dashed out, with a thousand kinds of killing. In the chase, all, for the most part, were killed either in the head or neck, for our horsemen," lie adds regretfully, "could not well reach them lower with their swords; and thus, with blood and slaughter, the chase continued for five miles, from the fallow fields of Inveresk unto Edinburgh Park, and well-nigh to the gates of the town itself, in all of which space the dead bodies lay as thick as cattle grazing in a full-replenished pasture. The river

Esk was red with blood, so that in the same chase were counted, by some of our men who diligently observed it, as by several of the prisoners, who greatly lamented the result, upwards of 14,000 slain. It was a wonder to see how soon the dead bodies were stripped quite naked, whereby the persons of the enemy might be easily viewed. For tallness of stature, cleanness of skin, largeness of bone, and due proportion, I could not have believed there were so many in all their country."

In the place where the English cavalry were routed he records that they found their horses gored and hewed to pieces, and their slain riders so dreadfully gashed and mangled that their faces were undistinguishable. "Little Preston was found there with both his hands cut off by the wrists, and known to be him, for he wore on each arm a bracelet of gold. Edward Shelly, that worthy gentleman and gallant officer, lay among them pitifully disfigured, mangled, and only discernible by his beard."

And all this miserable slaughter had ensued to gratify the ambitious spirit of a dead king, who from his deathbed had bequeathed, like the first Edward to his successors, the hopeless task of attempting to coerce a free and warlike people.

Somerset did not follow up his success, or seek to pursue Arran, who retreated towards Stirling. To be ransomed, the Lord Chancellor, the Earl of Huntly, and 1,500 other prisoners, were sent on board the fleet; together with 30,000 suits of mail that were found on the field, or packed in cases in the camp. Besides "their common manner of armour" were found what Master Patten calls "certain nice instruments for war - nue boardes endes, about a foot in breadth and half a yarde in length, having on the inside handels made very cunningly of two cordes endes. These, O God's name! were their targettes against the shot of our small artillerie, for they were not able to hold cannon." In the tents, he adds, were found abundance of good provisions, white bread, ale, oat cakes, oatmeal, mutton, butter in pots, and cheese, and in the tents of the nobles good wine and silver plate.

Cold in the cause of their country, many of those same nobles, had been among the first to fly "like traitors," as Arran called them ; and hence came the rhyme, by which the Scots sought to console themselves for their defeat -

"'Twas English gold and Scots traitors won
Pinkie field, but no Englishman."

The Highlanders suffered little loss, they threw themselves into one dense circle, and in that strange order retired over the most difficult ground, where none could pursue them.

After remaining a week near Edinburgh, during which he burned Sir Andrew Barton's house in Leith, set fire to that town, and stripped the lead off Holyrood Church, the Protector Somerset commenced his retreat for England, having won a battle for no use or purpose; and the young Queen of Scots became the bride of France. Sir John Hayward's assertion, that Somerset lost only "under sixty men" in the whole sixteen days' campaign, must be treated as absurd.

As the English marched home by the field of Pinkie, they found the greater part of the dead still lying unburied. A number had been interred in St. Michael's Churchyard at Inveresk, in graves that were lightly turfed over. Beside several of the bodies, says Patten, there was set "a stick with a clout, a rag, an old shoe, or some other mark," by their sorrowing kindred, to distinguish them when they might come to inter them on the English leaving the country.

The day of this defeat was long remembered as the Black Saturday of Pinkie; but the English invariably named the battle after the adjacent town. Thus, in Bunbury Church, Cheshire, there is a monument to Sir George Beeston, who was knighted by Queen Elizabeth for his bravery against the Armada, and who died in 1601, at the age of 102 years. He fought in that great slaughter of the 10th of September, 1547, as his tomb records, *"contra Scotos apud Musselborrow."*

In the following "acquittance," rendered into English, it is styled the battle of Inveresk: - "I, Walter Scott, of Branxholm, knight, grant me to have received from an honourable man, Sir Patrick Cheyne, of Essilmont, knight, the sum of eight score English nobles - for which I was bound and obliged to content, and pay to Thomas Dacre, of Lanercost, knight, Englishman - taken of the said Sir Patrick, at the field of Inveresk, for his ransom; for which sum I hold me well content and payed. In witness whereof I have subscribed this, my letter of acquittance with my hand, at Edinburgh, this 2nd March, 1548" (Aberdeen Collections).

The result of Pinkie added greatly to the ferocity of subsequent encounters between the English and Scots, and the latter, on the borders, made the most dreadful retaliations, leading for a time to an inextinguishable thirst for blood.

SIEGE OF LEITH, 1560

N O MILITARY event of importance occurred during the short life of Edward VI or the subsequent reign of his sister Mary; and, prior to the exploits of Hawkins and Drake, the defence of the seaport of Leith by a French garrison, under a' Marshal of France, until compelled by hunger to eat their horses, when besieged by a mixed force of English and Scots, forms the next prominent occurrence in our warlike history.

The flame of the Reformation, long stifled in Scotland, had now burst forth and spread over the realm with the fury of a volcanic eruption. Elizabeth, then on the throne of England, had composed the dissensions of that kingdom; and finding her power there firmly established, she naturally turned her attention to Scotland, where the Catholic party would have formed but a minority, save for the power of the Queen Regent, Mary of Guise and Lorraine, and the presence of the French troops, who had been sent there to uphold the authority of Mary, her daughter, the Queen of Scotland and Consort of France. Elizabeth, though anxious enough to make some profit out of the troubles of the Scots, was too cunning, or too politic, to do much that might embroil her with France; but she supplied the enemies of the Regent with money and encouragement in secret. After the disgraceful demolition of the cathedrals, churches, and monasteries by the lawless mobs of Scotland, the Regent came to an open rupture with the Lords of the Congregation, as the insurgent nobles termed themselves, and both parties appealed to arms. Powerful reinforcements were expected by her from France, and on the 30th of July she formed a camp on the common still known as the Links of Leith, a town which the French forces - some of whom had been long in Scotland - now began to fortify, by adding to the defences erected there ten years before by André de Montalembert and General d'Essé d'Epainvilliers.

The council of the Protestant lords suspended the Queen Regent from the exercise of her office, but found themselves unable to reduce Leith, where the French soldiers, being veterans of Francis I and Henry II, gave infinite trouble to the less skilful levies of the Congregation, which blockaded the town in October, 1559. Before proceeding to extremities, they sent a long-winded summons, in the names of "their sovereign lord and lady Francis and Mary, King and Queen of Scotland and France," demanding that all "Scots and Frenchmen, of whatever estate or degree, depart out of the town of Leith within the space of twelve hours."

No answer was returned. The Regent, whose power was now over, lay ill on her death-bed, in the castle of Edinburgh, and the assailants prepared to attack the last remnant of her adherents in Leith, which they endeavoured to carry by assault; but their scaling-ladders proved too short, and the fire of the French repulsed them. The lords were short of money, and on losing 4,000 crowns of the sum sent by Queen Elizabeth for their aid, but which were abstracted, sword in hand, from the bearer by the Earl of Bothwell, their troops became disheartened, irresolute, and disorderly, despising alike the threats of the peers and the denunciations of the preachers.

In their disputation, they sent certain delegates to England, and a meeting was held at Berwick between the Duke of Norfolk and these persons, who were the Lord James Stuart (afterwards the Regent Murray), Patrick Ruthven (the ghastly Ruthven of the Rizzio murder), James Wishart, of Pittarrow, and three others. With these Reformers the Duke of Norfolk concluded a treaty, which, with some slight alterations, was confirmed by the Queen of England. The chief object of this treaty was the defence of the Protestant religion and of the ancient rights and liberties of Scotland against the attempts of France to destroy them and make a conquest of that kingdom - in effect, to crush completely the Catholic interest and the power of the House of Guise.

While these arrangements were pending, the French troops, under General d'Oisel, the Count de Martigues, and others, were ravaging Fife and destroying the estates of the leading Protestant lords, though closely followed and harassed by a body of cavalry, under Sir William Kirkaldy, of Grange, who sent a challenge to D'Oisel, defying him to mortal combat - an invitation which the Frenchman declined to accept. When marching eastward, on the 25th of March, 1560, the French ravagers reached the promontory of Kincraigie, in Fifeshire, where they "discerned eight great ships of the first rate at sea;" and concluding that these must have on board the long-expected succours from France, under the Marquis d'Elboeuf; in honour of this arrival, they fired seaward a salute from their great culverins on the brow of the bluff. Their *feu de joie* and congratulations were somewhat premature, as the strange barques proved to be the English fleet, commanded by Vice-Admiral William Winter, Master of the Naval Ordnance, sailing up the Firth to assist the Scottish lords in the reduction of Leith. On discovering St. George's Cross, the French, overwhelmed with mortification and disappointment, broke into three separate columns, and retreated westward towards Stirling, there to cross the river and regain their shelter in Leith. Death and disaster were the concomitants of this retreat, for Kirkaldy and others followed them closely, till they reached the seaport, harassed, palled with excesses, and minus some of the best and bravest of their comrades, among whom they regretted none so much as a Swiss captain named L'Abast, whose skull had been cloven, through steel and bone, by the sword of the Master of Lindesay, near Kinghorn. Coligny, the Seigneur d'Andelot, and Paul de la Barthe, Lord of Thermes, and Maréchal of France in 1555, also served in these Scottish wars.

In fulfilment of the treaty with England, when the winter snows melted and the season for action came, on the 2nd of April, 1560, there marched into Scotland an English force, amounting to 1,250 horse and 6,000 infantry, under the veteran William, Lord Grey of Wilton, Warden of the East and Middle Marches of England. The second officer in command was Sir James Crofts; the Lord Scrope was earl-marshal; Sir George Howard was general of the men-at-arms, and Burnaby Fitzpatrick was his lieutenant; Sir Henry Piercy was general of the light horse or demi-lances; Thomas Huggins was provost-marshal; William Pelham was captain of the pioneers (Stow); and Thomas Gower was captain of the ordnance.

The spread of the use of fire-arms had now led to some alteration in the military equipments of this period. Armour now seldom came below the hip, complete suits being only used for tilting; and knights frequently appeared in the lists without greaves or steel boots. The breastplates were made, however, much thicker, in order to be bullet-proof; the tassettes were now of one plate each, but marked as if composed of several; the point of the tapul projected downward, like the doublets of Elizabeth's time; and the morions were frequently beautifully embossed, especially those which came from France and Italy. Carbines, petronels, and dragons are frequently mentioned among the fire-arms of the age. The first was so named from having been first used in the vessels called carabs; the second from being fired with its square butt planted upon the chest; the third from its muzzle being frequently decorated with a dragon's head; and hence the troopers who used it came subsequently to be named dragoons. The wheel-lock hackbut was used in

Elizabeth's reign, with the rest for the heavy matchlock. But the powder was now made up in cases, each containing a complete charge, to facilitate the loading of the piece; and the strap to which they were attached was named a collar or bandolier. The lighter troops, called demi-lances, were now replacing the heavily mailed men-at-arms, who had figured so conspicuously in all wars since the Middle Ages.

In a letter of Sir John Harrington's, we find the pay and the clothing of Elizabeth's troops detailed at some length. The following is the outfit for an officer of the English service in 1599:-

"A cassock of broadcloth	£1	7	7
A doublet of canvas, with silk lining and buttons	0	14	5
Two shirts and two bands	0	9	6
Three pairs of stockings, at 2/4 each	0	7	0
Three pairs of shoes, at ditto	0	7	0
One pair of Venetians (i.e, long hose), with silver lace	0	15	4
Total	£4	0	10"

The prevailing colours for the clothing of this time were white and "sadd grene or russet," according to Grose, and red cloaks were worn chiefly by the cavalry. On the 23rd July, 1601 we find that when 1,500 of Elizabeth's soldiers arrived from England to share in the siege of Ostend, they wore red cassocks. Of these, says Stow, 1,000 were Londoners, and they are now represented by the 3rd Regiment of Foot, or Kentish Buffs.

On the day after Lord Grey of Wilton's forces entered Scotland, he marched as far as Dunglass, where the infantry encamped, while the cavalry - some of whom had served at Pinkie - were peacefully cantoned in the adjacent villages. The next day's march brought them to Haddington. As they had passed the castle of Dunbar, some of the Queen Regent's adherents sallied out; an encounter took place, and some lives were lost The third day's march brought them to Prestonpans, where they met the Scottish leaders, and had an interview; which is, perhaps, the more important from the fact that now we find, for the first time in history, Scottish and English forces acting together as allies.

Mary of Guise still remained obstinate. She would bow to no terms, and refused to dismiss the French troops without the consent of her daughter and the King of France. The English and Scots now advanced upon Leith, where the operations of the siege were inaugurated by a long and fierce skirmish, in which 900 French arquebusiers, under the Comte de Martigues, held the lanes and fields about Restalrig for several hours, but were at last driven from their posts after severe losses, and had to take shelter in Leith, against which the English placed their ordnance in position, first at the eminence known as the Hawkhill. In the skirmish referred to, young Piercy, son of the leader of the demi-lances, is said to have evinced the most distinguished bravery.

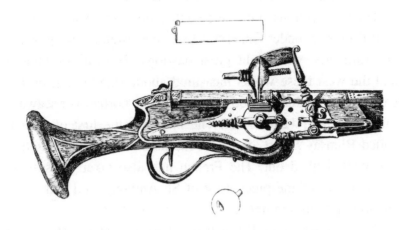

Breech-loading wheel-lock pistol (about time of Henry VIII).
Stock of ivory.

The French in Leith were now reduced to 5,000 men, and their orders were to defend the place to the last. The long-expected reinforcements, under René", the Marquis d'Elboeuf, uncle of the young Queen of Scotland and general of the galleys of France, never reached its shores. They were chiefly levied by the Rhinegrave's assistance (Camden); but a tempest scattered his fleet on the coast of Holland, and the little force in Leith was left to its own resources. It was now led by Monsieur Octavius, brother of D'Elbceuf, who was a peer of the house of Lorraine, and had led into Scotland some of the old Bandes Francaises; the Comte de Martigues, a young noble of the house of Luxembourg, afterwards Due d'Estampes and colonel-general of the infantry of France; Captain the Sieur Jacques de la Brosse, one of the hundred Knights of St. Michael; General d'Oisel, and other French officers of rank : but the senior there was the Florentine, Pietro Strozzi, Lord of Epernay (one of whose brothers, Gaspar, was killed at the storming of Inchkeith; another, Leon Strozzi, was Prior of Capua and general of the galleys of France at the siege of St. Andrews), and whose diploma as Marshal of France was issued in 1554, six years before the siege of Leith.

The fortifications of the latter at this time, chiefly made by the skilful French, under General d'Essé, consisted of strong walls and ramparts, with eight great bastions. Towards Edinburgh and the west these works measured about 16,500 feet; on the eastward more than 10,000 feet, and on the northern or seaward line more than 12,500 feet. The bastions, the first of which, called Ramsay's Fort, defended the harbour, were all angular, and well flanked out. The French had also taken possession of the tower of the preceptory of St. Anthony, and had slung cannon up to its summit.

The English, says Holinshed, began to cut trenches; and raised a mound, which they called Mount Pelham, on the south-east side of the town, for a battery of cannon. Lord Grey, with the demi-lances, occupied the little town of Restalrig, and to the north of it the infantry, "with their captains, were lodged in halls, huts, and pavilions." In this camp were the Earls of Montrose, Argyle, Glencairn, the Prior of St. Andrews, and other Reformers, with only 2,000 men (though some accounts swell them up to 12,006), a fact which shows the total dislike of the mass of the people, either to the matter in hand, or to co-operation with English troops. Prior to the siege being opened, the French resorted to a little act of treachery.

Strozzi sent a special message to Lord Grey, requesting a "cessation of hostilities," which his lordship granted. Taking advantage of this, the French issued forth, and flocked in considerable numbers, and all with their arms, about the English encampments at Restalrig, Hawkhill, and Hermitage, affecting to be lured there by curiosity; while several concealed themselves in thickets and bushes. Some jostled the English sentinels, to provoke a challenge or quarrel; and when Lord Grey, disliking these demonstrations, ordered them to retire, their reply was that "they should like to know his right to order them off the ground of their mistress, the Queen Regent." They were then told that "had it not been for the cessation of hostilities granted at their own request, they would have been compelled to keep at a respectful distance." This answer irritated the French, who, after defying the English to "do their worst," deliberately fired their arquebuses and pistols point-blank into the faces of those who were nearest to them.

A volley of English oaths followed this treacherous attack, and a conflict instantly ensued. Those French who were in concealment now rushed to join their comrades. The English, taken thus completely by surprise, were thrown into confusion, and were seen running to arms in all directions, and yet none in camp knew whence came the dreadful uproar. At every turn they were met and slaughtered by the French; and shouts now mingled with the incessant explosion of arquebuses, till the French were driven in pell-mell through one of the gates of Leith, with the loss of 140 men killed, and twelve gentlemen and five arquebusiers taken prisoners. The loss of the English is not recorded, but we may reasonably conclude that, as they were attacked unawares, it would exceed that of their assailants.

The position of the English, on the rising ground extending to Hermitage Hill, was sufficiently commanding and well chosen, but was too remote to enable the artillery of those days to injure either the town or its fortifications. They spent the first few days of the siege in forming bulwarks arid digging trenches to protect themselves from the spirited arid incessant sallies of the French. Whenever they perceived any detachments advancing from the town, an equal force was sent to meet them. These parties generally met midway on the Links of Leith, and there many encounters of a sanguinary nature ensued.

Tiring of this, and to press the siege, Lord Grey formed batteries nearer the walls - one, named Mount Pelham, already mentioned, at the distance of 1,200 feet from the eastern ramparts; one, named Mount Somerset, at 600 feet distance; and a third, named Mount Falcon, at 250 feet southeast of St. Ninian's Church - and it is interesting to observe that two of these mounds still remain; arid from their summits may still be traced the zig-zags, or regular approaches made to the walls by the soldiers of Elizabeth.

After a cannonade for several days from eight guns on Mount Somerset, the steeple of St Anthony, with its cannon and defenders, fell with a mighty crash. This feat, which a single shot from some of our modern cannon would accomplish in one minute, afforded the greatest exultation to the gunners of Captain Pelham, "who actually contemplated with wonder the effect of their prowess." Admiral Winter's fleet now seconded the efforts of the besiegers, by sailing close to the pier, where the crews opened a most destructive fire, by which many of the soldiers and of the luckless inhabitants were killed and wounded.

Thomas Churchyard, the English poet, was one of Lord Grey's soldiers, and among his "Chips" is a poem entitled "The Siege of Leith; more aptly called, The Schole of Warre." It was printed at London, in 1565, and contains many curious details.

On the 21st of April, Jean de' Monluc, the learned Bishop of Valence, in Savoy, 'came as ambassador to Scotland. He was conveyed first to the English camp, and thence to the castle of Edinburgh, where for two days, he held a conference with the Queen Regent, without effecting the object of his mission - a peaceful reconciliation, with the dismissal of the French troops, who were already suffering from lack of supplies.

On the 4th of May an attempt was made to carry the town by storm; and the "Orders for Thassalt" (sic), issued by Lord Grey, are curious, as being, perhaps, one of the oldest detailed orders extant, and containing the names of some of the earliest

Incident in the Siege of Leith.

officers in the English army: "May 4, 1560, vppone Saturdaye, in the mornyng, at thri of the clock, God willinge, we shalbe in readynes to give the assalte, in order as followithe, if other ympedyment than we knowe not yet of hyndre us not."

For the first assault were detailed Captain Rede, with 300 men; Captains Markham, Taxley, Sutton, Fairfax, Mallorye, the Provost - Marshal, Aston, Conway, Drury (afterwards Sir William Drury, Marshal of Berwick), Berkeley, and Fitzwilliams, each with 200 men, and 500 arquebusiers to be furnished by the Scots. For the second assault, fourteen captains and 2,240 men. "To kepe the fielde," Captain Somerset and eight other captains, with 2,400 men. To be furnished by "the Vyce-Admyralle of the Quene's Majesty's Schippes," 500 men. Captain Vaughan was to assault the town near Mount Pelham, and the Scots on the seaward.

The attack on four quarters of the town was not made till seven in the morning. The fleet failed to send the required men, thus enabling the French to muster at the points assailed with greater strength. The scaling-ladders proved too short by half a pike's length. Sir James Crofts committed some terrible blunders; and as he had lately had an interview with the Queen Regent, "appeared to act under enchantment." The whole attempt turned out a failure, and the English were repulsed with slaughter, and driven out of their trenches by the Comte de Martigues, to the risk of having their cannon taken. Pitscottie says 100 of "the English white cloakes" were slain. Keith has it that, in scouring the trenches, the French slew 600 men, spiked three pieces of cannon - and captured Sir Maurice Berkeley, adds Camden.

The siege had continued nearly a month, without any prospect of a termination; and hitherto it had been attended with no other effect (exclusive of the daily loss of life, especially as Elizabeth continued to send more troops and ships) than of reducing the garrison to such dire extremity for want of provisions, that they were compelled to shoot and eat the horses of the officers and gens d'armes. Yet they endured their privations with true French *sang-froid*, vowing never to surrender while a horse was left; "their officers exhibiting that politeness in the science of gastronomy which is recorded of the Maréchal Strozzi, whose *maître de cuisine*, during the blockade, maintained his master's table with twelve covers every day, although he had nothing better to set upon it now and then except the quarter of a carrion horse, dressed with the grass and weeds which grew upon the ramparts."

The repulse of the assault, in which we are told the French were assisted by their "Scottish paramours," who fired arquebuses, and threw burning coals, stones, and timber on the stormers, greatly exasperated the English; but still more did a display of the dead bodies of their comrades, whom the French stripped quite nude, and barbarously arrayed in grotesque order on the slope of the glacis towards Lord Grey's camp - a display which John Knox pretends the Queen Regent could see, and exult over, from the castle of Edinburgh.

The unfortunate princess was sinking fast, and now requested an interview with General d'Oisel, her friend and countryman, who was shut up in Leith. This, of course, was denied her. She then wrote to him, " telling him how heavily the hand of death now pressed upon her," and begging certain medicines. But this letter was intercepted by Lord Grey of Wilton.

"Here lurketh some mystery," said the wary old veteran, as he viewed the letter in various ways, "for medicines are more abundant in Edinburgh than in Leith."

On holding it before a fire some secret writing appeared, on which he threw it into the flames.

"Albeit, I have been thus her secretary," said he, "I shall keep her counsel, yet say unto her such wares will not sell until there be a new market."

Mary did not live to see the fall of Leith, as she died in the castle of Edinburgh, on the 10th of June, utterly worn out by sickness and grief.

Fresh reinforcements having come to enforce the siege (Sir James Balfour states in his Annals that by the time the horses were all eaten, the blockading force of the Lords of the Congregation amounted to "12,000 Scotts Protestants," commanded by the Duke of Chatelherault, eleven peers, and 120 lesser barons), the queen being dead, and their cause desperate, the French garrison began to think of capitulating. A treaty of peace was framed, including England, Scotland, and France, and by this treaty, which was signed at Edinburgh, it was stipulated that the French should be allowed to embark for France, without molestation, with bag and baggage, on board of English ships; and that the English forces should commence their homeward march on the day the French evacuated the town. It was expressly stipulated that an officer and sixty men of the latter should remain in the castle of Inchkeith, for what use we cannot now see.

Accordingly, on the 16th day of July, 1560, the French troops, after plundering Leith of all that they could lay their hands upon, marched out, 4,000 strong, and embarked under Marshal Strozzi, on board of the queen's English ships, after having served in Scotland for nearly fourteen years.

At the same hour the troops of Lord Grey began their march for the borders, and were accompanied as a mark of respect by many Lords of the Congregation. A solemn thanksgiving was held in the church of St. Giles, where the services were conducted by John Knox. After the conclusion of these important transactions, the safety of Berwick became a matter of serious consideration to the English Court, and its garrison was ordered to consist permanently of the strength of 2,000 men.

Besides the battery-mounds, which still remain at Leith and the trenches yet visible, many relics of this siege are often discovered there. In the *Scotsman* of 1857 and 1859 are reported the exhuming of several skeletons buried in the vicinity of these old earthworks; and many human bones, cannon balls, old swords, &c, have been dug up from time to time in the immediate vicinity of the street called Wellington Place. Two of the principal thoroughfares were long known by the name of "Les Deux Bras," being so styled by the garrison of Mary of Guise.

- C H A P T E R   V I -
ZUTPHEN, 1586

IN TRACING British military achievements through a series of historiettes, we have now arrived at the epoch of the two cousins, Elizabeth and Mary, an age rightly distinguished as "the Elizabethan;" the age in which the naval glory of England shone out so brilliantly - in which the Portuguese, the Dutch, and Castilians had led the way to unknown seas and shoves, and England was not far behind them; for Sir Francis Drake sailed round the world, Sir Martin Frobisher braved the terrors of the Arctic Sea, Sir John Hawkins traced out the burning coast of Guinea, and Sir Walter Raleigh colonised America, and named his settlement Virginia, in compliment to his queen.

Though the latter preferred peace, she was not afraid of war; and when the United Provinces, in their sore extremity, had recourse to her for protection, she concluded a treaty with them, in consequence of which she was put in possession of the Brille, Flushing, and the castle of Ramakins, as security for the payment of her expenses. She knew that the step she had taken would immediately engage her in hostilities with Philip II of Spain, whose bigotry and misgovernment had produced such distress and dissension in the Netherlands, to the heritage of which he had succeeded, like Maximilian of Austria, as a portion of the possessions of the Duke of Burgundy. But the power of Philip did not alarm her, though such prepossessions were everywhere prevalent of the vast force of the Spanish monarchy that the King of Sweden, when informed that the Queen of England had openly embraced the cause of the revolted Flemings, said, "She has now taken the diadem from her head, and placed it on the point of a sword;" and still more did it look like this when the terrible Armada came to be spoken of.

On the 10th of December, 1585, the English armament arrived off Flushing, of which Sir Philip Sidney was already governor. It was under the command of Robert Dudley, Earl of Leicester, K.G., who had been rejected by the Queen-of the Scots, and now aspired to the hand of Elizabeth; a man who in private life was little esteemed, and in his public character detested as the murderer of Amy Robsart. The queen had bound o send a fleet of forty ships, the least of which should be forty tons; but now this fleet consisted of fifty sail, chiefly hired merchant ships, having on board 6,000 men. With Dudley were the Earls of Essex, Oxford, and Northumberland; Lords Willoughby, Audley, Sheffield, K.B., Burroughs, and North; Sir Thomas Shirley, Sir Arthur Basset, Sir Gervase Clifton, Sir Philip, Sir Robert, and Sir Henry Sidney, and many other knights, together with a select troop' of 500 gentlemen. The latter served at their own' expense, as volunteers, and among them was Sir Francis de Vere, one of the most gallant soldiers of the age, and the lineal descendant of Alaric de Vere, who came over with William the Conqueror.

By the revolted Flemings, Leicester was received as a guardian angel; and, by way of expressing their gratitude to his sovereign, they immediately made him Governor and Captain-General of Holland, Zealand, and the United Provinces, investing him with absolute power. He was attended by a noble guard, and saluted by all men with the title of "Your Excellency," upon which, adds Camden, "he began to take upon him as if he were a perfect king."

Leicester possessed neither, courage nor capacity to fulfil the trust reposed in him; and he speedily showed his inability to direct military operations by permitting the Duke of Parma to advance in a rapid course of conquests, and abused his authority by a course of administration, wanton and cruel, weak yet oppressive.

At this period companies of infantry in all European armies varied from 150 to 300 men, and each company had a colour or ensign, and the mode of formation recommended by Sir John Smith, an English military writer of those days, was that the colours should be in the centre invariably, and guarded by the halberdiers; for under Elizabeth every company consisted of men armed in five different ways. In every hundred men, forty were men-at-arms, and sixty "shot." The former were ten halberdiers and thirty pikemen. Bruce, in his "Military Law, 1717," says, the tallest men were always "culled out for that service." The "shot" were twenty archers, twenty musketeers, and twenty arquebusiers, and, in addition to his principal weapon, every man carried a sword and dagger.

20	20	20	30	20	30	20	20	20
Arquebuses.	Archers.	Muskets.	Pikes.	Halberts.	Pikes.	Muskets.	Archers.	Arquebuses.

According to the tactics of the time, the formation of a single company in line would appear as above.

It was customary to unite these companies into one body, called a regiment, frequently amounting to 3,000 men. The muskets carried a ball weighing one-tenth of a pound; the arquebuse a ball weighing one-twenty-fifth of a pound. The ancient war-cry was still retained, as it was enacted that all soldiers entering into battle, assault, skirmish, or other faction of arms, shall have for their common cry "Saint George, forward!" or, "Upon them, Saint George!" At this time the rank of sergeant-major, then the same as adjutant, first appears.

No great battle, but little more than a series of skirmishes, some of which were brilliant in their way, distinguished the expedition of Leicester to the Low Countries. He suffered the Prince of Parma to besiege and capture Greve, or Graves,

Venloo, and other places, and then to pass the Rhine, after which he threw succours into Zutphen.

At Greve the English infantry were commanded by the Lord of Van Hernert, a Dutchman, says Cardinal Bentivoglio, in his "History of Flanders," and formed its garrison when besieged by the Spaniards under the Prince of Parma. "The enemy strove to capture the place, and Leicester prepared to relieve it. For that purpose he sent out a good proportion of horse and foot; and the king's men were not wanting in making such opposition as was needful, though they had not men enough to keep the garrison from making excursions, and hinder the designs which the enemy had without. During this uncertainty of the siege on one side, and of the succour on the other, there happened divers actions and skirmishes, one of which proved very bloody. The English intended to relieve the town chiefly by the way of a great dyke that ran along the Maese, and for this purpose had fortified themselves upon it, and prepared divers barques upon the river. Wherefore, taking their time, they began to march with some squadrons of foot, and advanced boldly. The Royalists (i.e., the Spaniards) were very watchful on their part; and, resolving to repulse the succour, likewise marched boldly to the encounter. The conflict was very hot for a time, tilt the English began to give way and retreat, which made the King of Spain's men press forward the more eagerly; but being too enthusiastic in their pursuit, they fell into disorder, and while in this state were suddenly attacked by a fresh body of English infantry, and routed with great slaughter."

The English were commanded by Sir Francis Vere, and the Spaniards were the brigade of Don Juan d'Aquila, who there lost seven captains, among other officers, and 200 soldiers. The English failed to capture another dyke, of which the Spaniards had possessed themselves; but the repulse of Aquila, a *maestro de campo*, enabled them to succour their countrymen in the town, by means of some boats on the Maese, and thus protract the defence, a result which exasperated the Prince of Parma, who ordered Altapenna to relinquish the siege of Nuys, and bring his troops to Greve. Fresh trenches were dug and battenes erected, and twenty-four pieces of heavy artillery were opened upon the town. The Earl of Leicester, on whom the hopes of the beseiged rested, had already advanced to Utrecht, and thence to Amheim, but there he halted. On this "the Lord of Hemert, with some of his captains, being poorly timorous, began to treat for a surrender. Nor could the prince refuse them any conditions they could desire, that he might the sooner rid his hands of the enterprise."

The garrison had made a brave defence, and the troops were permitted to march out with bag and baggage, arms and armour, and with colours flying ; but the Prince of Parma repented that he had not taken them all prisoners of war, for the moment they reached the camp of the Earl of Leicester, that noble, in virtue of his authority as governor and captain-general, mercilessly put the Lord of Hemert, "and all the captains that partook with him in the surrender, to an ignominious death."

After the fall of Greve, Sir Francis and his company distinguished themselves at the escalade of Avil. Some brilliant services were also performed by his friend and comrade, Sir Philip Sidney. The latter, on his arrival in Zealand, had formed a close friendship and intimacy with Maurice, son of the Prince of Orange, and in conjunction with him entered Flanders, and took Axel, in Zealand, by surprise. Though local historians always name the prince only in this enterprise, the honour of the contrivance and the execution of it are ascribed by the English to the gallant Sidney, who revived the ancient discipline of perfect silence on the march, and by this conduct his soldiers were enabled to approach the walls unheard, and to scale them in the night, when no attack was expected. Having succeeded in this, a chosen band made directly for the court-of-guard, in the market-place, took the officers prisoners, and thus the victors became masters of Axel before the Spanish commandant, who had the keys of the town under his pillow, had the least idea it was taken.

Encouraged by this success, Sidney made an attempt on Gravelines, but the design failed, through some treachery on the part of an officer named La Motte.

On the Prince of Parma, the brilliant Alexander Famese, marching to Rhineburg, which was held by a garrison of 1,200 Englishmen, under Colonel Morgan, the Earl of Leicester began to bestir himself. He, perhaps, felt shame at the conquests of the prince. He reinforced his army as much as he could, says Cardinal Bentivoglio, and resolved to relieve that town, or make some diversion by besieging one garrisoned by the King of Spain. He was on the other side of the Rhine, in the province of Overisel, so called because the Isel runs through it. On the right bank thereof stands Zutphen, a town then of the greatest importance, which Leicester hoped to reduce; but before doing so he resolved to take Doesburg, a small town upon the same river.

It was garrisoned by only 300 Walloons, who capitulated at the first cannon-shot; he then marched on to Zutphen. The city had a great earthen fort on the side which faced the river, and two smaller works, which aided in strengthening the place. The commander of the Spanish garrison was John Baptisti di Tessis, an Italian cavalier. He instantly dispatched messengers to the Prince of Parma, requiring succour, as he was short of provisions, and unable to endure a siege. Crossing the Rhine by a pontoon bridge, the prince marched at once towards the English. *En route* he was informed that 2,000 reiters had been raised on the confines of Germany by the Count de Meurs, to join Leicester, and that there was no time to be lost. He therefore selected 1,500 horse, mounted a Spanish arquebusier behind each rider, and sent them forward with all speed towards Zutphen, while he followed with his main body.

The advanced party fell in with the reiters of the count, who were not expecting an attack, and were easily cut to pieces; and, thereafter, pushing on, the prince prepared at the point of the sword to succour Zutphen. The Marquis of Vasto was ordered forward with some squadrons of Italian horse, and a body of Spanish, Italian, and Walloon infantry, as an escort to a long train of wagons laden with provisions for the city. The cavalry, who were in front of this formidable convoy, were suddenly assailed in a fog by those of Leicester, who charged them with so much force and fury that they were disordered and driven back. They rallied, but only to be driven back again by the English. A second time they rallied, and the conflict long remained doubtful.

The Marquis de Vasto displayed the greatest valour. The Italian troops, under the Marquis Hanibal de Gonzaga, the Marquis de Bentivoglio and Giorgio Cresso, fought with incredible ardour; but the last-named leader fell into the hands of the, English, and Gonzaga, an Italian noble, of high family and brilliant reputation, was unhorsed and mortally wounded. During the conflict the Prince of Parma came up, with his whole army in order of battle; upon which the Earl of Leicester, whose forces were no match for the more numerous Spaniards, ordered his trumpets to sound a retreat, and thus permitted Zutphen to be relieved.

At a future time he assaulted the earthen forts by which the town was defended, and one of the lesser was stormed and garrisoned by the English, under an officer named Rowland Yorke. It was during one of these conflicts before Zutphen that the episode occurred which made the name of Sir Philip Sidney so remarkable in history. He had signalised himself one day by prodigies of valour, for he was a warlike enthusiast of the highest order. Two horses had been killed under him, and he was in the act of mounting a third, when an arquebuse-shot from the trenches broke one of his thigh-bones. He was unable to manage his horse, but the faithful animal bore him out of the field to the camp, a mile and a half distant. He was in great agony, and faint from loss of blood, and when passing the rest of the army called for water. It was brought him, but as he was putting the bottle to his mouth, he saw a poor English soldier borne past who was more severely wounded than himself, and who gazed at the bottle longingly, and with haggard eyes.

"Thy necessity is yet greater than mine," said the gentle and heroic Sidney; nor would he drink until the soldier had been satisfied. He was then borne to Arnheim, where the principal surgeons were stationed. Hopes were entertained of his recovery for sixteen days; but as they were unable to extract the ball, and mortification ensued, he prepared to meet death, with a resignation, piety, and fortitude that corresponded to his past life; and he expired in the arms of his brother, Sir Robert Sidney, on the 17th of October, 1586, in the thirty-second year of his age. The United Provinces wished to have the care of his interment, but this was declined by Queen Elizabeth, by whose orders his body was embarked for England with the military honours of the time. It was received at the Tower of London in the same manner; and, after lying in state for some days, was solemnly interred in old St. Paul's. Besides his fame as a soldier, Sir Philip Sidney has left us an unfading memorial of his genius in his celebrated romance of "Arcadia." His patent to be Governor of Flushing was dated at Westminster, 9th November, 1585 (Rymer's "Fœdera"). The pedantic King of Scotland was so struck with admiration of Sidney's virtue that he celebrated his memory in Latin verses, which are but little known now.

It was in this war that shells were first thrown out of mortars, at the siege of Wachtendonk, by the Count of Mansfeld. They were first invented by a citizen of Venloo, who on a festival celebrated in honour of the Duke of Cleves, threw a certain number, one of which fell on a house and set fire to it, by which misfortune most of the city was reduced to ashes.

The Earl of Leicester, a man of great pride and ambition, is accused by the Dutch historians of aiming at sovereign power

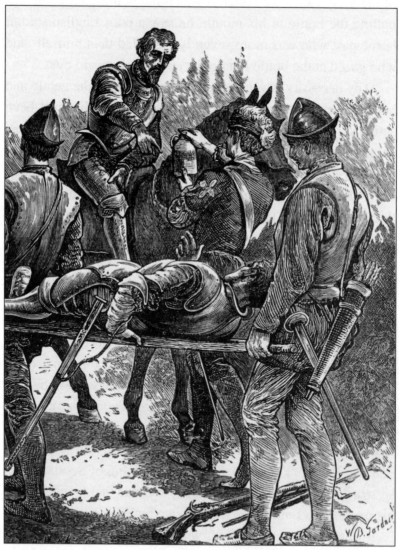

Sir Philip Sidney at Zutphen.

in the provinces he had come to free, and yet failed to achieve anything in their behalf. Colonel William Stanley, a Catholic, was colonel of an English regiment, 1,200 strong, that garrisoned the city of Deventer; but, in his zeal for religion, and dread of the result of the Babington conspiracy, he gave up the town to Tessis, the Governor of Zutphen, and joined the Spaniards with all his men, an example followed soon after by Rowland Yorke, who held the forts of Zutphen; so loss and treachery soon excited an outcry against Leicester, who was summoned to England, leaving Lord Willoughby to command the English forces in the Low Countries. Colonel Paton, a Scot, who held the town of Gueldres, fearing that his post would be bestowed upon an Englishman, about the same time surrendered it to the Spaniards.

"Were these the aids, were these the advantages, they expected from England?" exclaims Cardinal Bentivoglio. "Was this the fruit they reaped from the Earl of Leicester's government? On his coming into Flanders he made miracles to be expected at his hands; but how soon were those miracles turned into shame! How many places had the Duke of Parma taken, while he has looked on! And how much to his dishonour had he failed to relieve Zutphen! On leaving for England he had become the enemy of the Flemings, and had placed Englishmen wherever he pleased, in lieu of the native Flemish."

Zutphen eventually fell, through the generalship of Sir Francis Vere. Prince Maurice being about to advance towards it, Vere pushed forward with his own corps, sweeping the country of its cattle and forage to straiten the garrison. Adjoining the town stood a strong fort, the possession of which promised materially to forward the operations of a siege; but which on a former occasion had cost Leicester a heavy loss ere he succeeded in reducing it. Of this fort Vere resolved to make himself master, and he chose the following stratagem for the purpose.

Selecting certain young men of his corps, he appareled

them like Flemish countrywomen, and sent them forward with well-filled baskets on then-backs, but with swords, daggers, and loaded pistols under their aprons and fardingales. They travelled towards Zutphen in groups of two and three together, to elude observation, and about dawn of day found themselves close to the gate of the fort, where they sat down and deposited their baskets, as if waiting for a ferry-boat. No suspicion that they were other than that which they appeared to be, market-women, arose among the garrison. The Spanish soldiers opened the gates as usual, let down the bridge, and many came forth to converse with the country-people, who now ran to meet them, with loud laughter, till they gained the covered way. Then they drew their weapons, overpowered the barrier-guard, and maintained themselves in the archway till a body of troops, sent forward swiftly and silently by Vere to their support, came up. So the castle was taken, and Zutphen, which depended upon it as a principal bulwark, surrendered after a very feeble resistance ("History of the Republic of Holland," London, 1705).

The taking of Zutphen.

- C H A P T E R   V I I -

EXPLOITS OF SIR FRANCIS DRAKE

BY SEA, the attempts of Elizabeth to humble the Spaniards were much more successful and brilliant - than in the Low Countries. America was regarded as the chief source of the great wealth of Philip II., as well as the most defenceless portion of his vast dominions; and as a breach had now been made with him, Elizabeth was resolved not to leave him unmolested in that quarter. The great success of the Spaniards and Portuguese in both Indies had excited the emulation of the English; and as the progress of commerce - still more that of colonies - is slow, it was fortunate that a war at this critical period had opened a more flattering object to ambition and to avarice, by tempting England to engage in naval enterprises.

Drake and Hawkins were at this time in the zenith of their fame; but accounts differ very much as to the naval force of England. Some assert that the navy about the year 1578 consisted of 146 sail, whose guns varied from forty to six. Campbell, in his "Lives of the Admirals," discredits this statement; and the most accurate accounts we seem to have of the navy in the year named make it to consist of only twenty-four ships - the largest being the *Triumph*, of 1,000 tons, and the smallest the *George*, 60 tons. "The whole number of ships in England," says Captain Schomberg, R.N., "was estimated at this time at 135, from 100 tons upwards, and 650 from 40 to 100 tons." The queen dined on board the ship, the *Golden Hind*, in which Sir Francis Drake sailed round the world, and gave orders that it should be preserved as a lasting monument of his own and of England's glory; but in process of years she was broken up, and nothing now remains of her but a chair, which was presented to the University of Oxford.

The dinner occurred at Deptford, on the 4th of April, 1584, and on that occasion she knighted him. Drake, one of England's most eminent naval heroes, was born of humble parents, near Tavistock, in 1545. He was one of the twelve sons of Edmund Drake, a poor seaman, and in his nineteenth year was captain of the *Judith*, when he fought so gallantly under Sir John Hawkins, at San Juan de Ulloa, in the Gulf of Mexico.

Under Sir Francis, a fleet of twenty-one sail was prepared for an expedition to the West Indies. Besides the seamen, 2,300 soldiers, under Christopher, Earl of Carlisle, were put on board. Many of the latter were volunteers of spirit and enterprise, and all were led by well-trained officers; for, like the navy, the army was now becoming a regular profession. The land officers were Captain Anthony Powel, sergeant-major; Captains Morgan and Sampson, "corporals of the field;" and ten other captains. Drake's own ship was named the *Elizabeth Bonaventure*, Captain William Fenner. The *Great Galleon* was under Rear-Admiral Francis Knollys; Carlisle, lieutenant-general, was in the *Tiger*.

This expedition left England in March, 1585; and the reader may be able to form some idea of the names, dimensions, and weight of the cannon-shot, and powder of the ancient English ordnance from Sir William Morison, in his "Naval Tracts," written in the time of Elizabeth and James I. (See table on opposite page).

Bombardes were greatly used by the Spaniards and Portuguese on board of their great caracks; and M. Blondel, in his "Art de Jetter des Bombes," says, they were first used for shelling purposes in land war against Wachtendonck, in Gueldreland, in 1588.

The use of the explosive shell had at this time been known to the English for more than forty years. Stow tells us that, about 1543, Ralph Hogge, the Sussex gun - founder, brought over a certain Fleming, named Peter Van Collet, who "devised, or caused to be made, certain mortar pieces, being at the mouth from eleven to nine inches wide, for the use whereof the said Peter caused to be made certain hollow shot to be stuffed with fyrework, whereof the bigger sort for the same has screws of iron to receive a match to carry fyre, to break in small pieces the said hollow shot, whereof the smallest piece hitting a man would kill or spoil him."

Drake's first exploit in this voyage was to plunder Vigo, to the amount of 30,000 ducats, including a cross from the cathedral, of silver double gilt. His next was the surprise and capture of St. Jago, near the Cape de Verde. There he found plenty of provisions but no treasure, and after setting the town on fire he bore on for the West Indies; and after losing 300 men by disease at Dominica, in January, 1586, he was off the island of Hispaniola.

He landed with 1,200 pike-men and musketeers, and 200 seamen, within ten miles of the city of San Domingo, and when he drew near it there came forth 150 Spanish gentlemen, all well mounted and armed, to oppose him, but they were speedily

Name	Bore (Inches)	Weight of gun (lbs.)	Weight of shot (lbs.)	Weight of powder (lbs.)
Cannon-royale	8.5	8,000	66	30
Cannon	8	6,000	60	27
Serpentine	7	5,500	53.5	25
Bastard-Cannon	7	4,500	41	20
Demi-Cannon	6.75	4,000	30.5	18
Culverin	5.5	4,500	17.5	12
Basilisk	5	400	15	10
Saker	3.5	1,400	5.5	5.5
Falcon	2.5	660	2	3.5

Information taken from Sir William Morison's "Naval Tracts".

repulsed; and then the English advanced towards the two gates of the city, which then faced the sea. These barriers the Spaniards were resolved to defend, and had manned them both well.

In front of each they had planted some pieces of cannon, and placed arquebusiers in ambush on each side of the way; but Sir Francis Drake and a captain named Powell, each leading one-half of the force landed, marched resolutely against both gates at once, vowing that, "with God's assistance, they would not give over till they met each other in the market-place."

Sir Francis, having received the fire of both the cannon in front and the ambush on his flank, charged furiously to prevent them reloading. He captured the guns, put the Spaniards to flight, and entering the gate with the fugitives, pell-mell, soon cut a passage, as he had sworn, to the market - place, where Captain Powell, whose success at the other gate was exactly similar, met him soon after, with the survivors of his command.

There they barricaded themselves, because the town was too large to be overrun by a force so small as theirs; and about midnight they attacked the gate of the castle, upon which the Spaniards instantly abandoned it. Some of the garrison were made prisoners, and the rest fled seaward in boats. The English having now possession of the fortress, enlarged their quarters, and remained in San Domingo for a month. They were completely masters of the place, which an eye-witness of the expedition, whose narrative is preserved, describes as a city of great extent and magnificence, but which Drake wasted with fire and sword during the whole of January.

During that time he sent a negro boy with a flag of truce to the Spaniards. He was met by some officers of a galley which Drake had taken in the harbour, and one of them barbarously ran him through the body with his sword. The boy lived to crawl back and acquaint Sir Francis with this outrage, and then expired at his feet.

Upon this, in a very questionable spirit, Drake ordered his provost-marshal to hang two Spanish friars he had taken prisoners j and sent another to inform the Spanish officers that "until they delivered up to him the officer who murdered his messenger, he would hang two Spanish prisoners every day." The Spaniards thereupon found themselves compelled to send the officer; and Sir Francis forced the escort who brought him to hang him instantly in his presence.

These stern measures greatly terrified and exasperated the inhabitants of San Domingo, to whom he sent commissioners to treat about the ransom of the whole city from destruction; and, to make matters more speedy, as there was some delay in the transaction, he employed 200 seamen in the task of deliberately burning the place. But the houses being all of stone, and remarkably well built, they could not consume above one-third of it.

At. last the Spaniards agreed to give 25,000 ducats, value five shillings and sixpence each, that the portion of the city remaining might be 'spared. He carried off a vast quantity of rich apparel, linen, woollen, and silk stuffs, with wine, oil, vinegar, wheat, and store of china, but very little plate, and, save the ransom, no money of consequence, as the Spaniards had only copper, for want of hands to work the mines of silver and gold.

He next appeared off Carthagena, in New Andalusia, as it was then named. The harbour had two entrances, the chief of which lay half a league east-Ward from the city, and the other nearer, named La Bocachico. Both of these have ever been dangerous, on account of the many shallows at the entrance, causing the most careful steerage to be necessary. But though the city was fortified by many "sconces," or batteries, Sir Francis Drake sailed boldly in with his pinnaces, and took it by storm on the land side. He also captured two forts, one of which secured the mouth of the smaller entrance together with a boom. He took and plundered a great-Franciscan abbey that stood thereby, surrounded with strong walls. Here many of the English perished by wounds from poisoned arrows, and poisoned spikes which were stuck in the earth. He completely pillaged Carthagena, set it on fire, and would have destroyed it completely, had it not been ransomed by the neighbouring colonies for the sum of 120,000 ducats.

San Antonio and Santa Elena, on the coast 61 Florida, shared the fate of Carthagena; and soon after he appeared off San Augustine - a little town with a castle, in the province of Sagasta, near the river May, upon a pleasant hill covered with fine trees. Fort St. John defended the town, which was almost square, with four streets, composed entirely of wooden houses.

Fort St. John was octagonal, with a round tower at each corner. Drake instantly attacked it, upon which the garrison fled, abandoning £2,000 in a treasure-ship, and fourteen pieces of brass cannon, all of which were sent off to the fleet, which, after pillaging and burning the town, bore along the coast of Virginia, where Sir Francis found the small remains of the colony which Sir Walter Raleigh had planted there, and which had gone to extreme decay. The poor planters implored Drake to take them back with him to England, to which he returned with so much riches that privateering became greatly encouraged; and he brought such accounts of the weakness and cowardice of the Spaniards, that the spirit of the nation became inflamed for further enterprise. Even the great mortality which the climate had produced in his fleet - which lost 700 men - the result also of excess and meagre medical arrangements - was but a slender restraint on the avidity and sanguine hopes of young adventurers. Ralph Lane, one of the Virginian colonists who came home with Drake, is said by Camden to have been the first man who brought the tobacco-leaf to England. The fleet came to anchor in- Portsmouth Harbour on the 28th of July, 1586.

Drake brought back with him to England plunder to the value of £60,000 sterling, with 240 brass and iron cannon; and the fame of this induced a gentleman of Devonshire, named Thomas Cavendish, who had dissipated a good estate by living at Court, to seek his fortune, sword in hand, among the Spaniards. He fitted out three ships at Plymouth, one of 120 tons, another of 60 tons, and a third of 40 tons, and with these small vessels he had the hardihood to sail for the southern seas, where he committed terrible depredations. He took no less than nineteen Spanish vessels, richly laden; and returning by the Cape of Good Hope, he came to London, where he sailed up the Thames in a kind of picturesque triumph. His mariners and soldiers were all clothed in silk of the most brilliant colours his sails were of damask, his topsail was glittering cloth of gold, and the prizes were the richest that had as yet been brought to England.

But now Elizabeth, on hearing that Philip of Spain, though he seemed to dissemble, or to ignore the daily insults and injuries sustained by his flag from the English, was equipping a great navy to attack her, ordered Sir Francis Drake once more to prepare for sea.

These equipments ultimately developed themselves as the Great Armada; but the arrangements were so vast that Sir Francis Drake says in one of his letters, quoted by Strype, that the Spaniards had provisions of bread and wine alone sufficient to maintain 40,000 men for a whole year. And that these preparations were aimed against England was discovered by Walsingham in a very singular manner. On learning that Philip had dispatched an express to Rome with a secret letter, written by his own hand, to the Pope, Sixtus V., "acquainting him with the true design in hand, and asking his blessing upon it;" Walsingham, by means of a Venetian priest, retained by him as a spy upon the Vatican, got a transcription of the original, which was abstracted from the Pope's cabinet by a gentleman

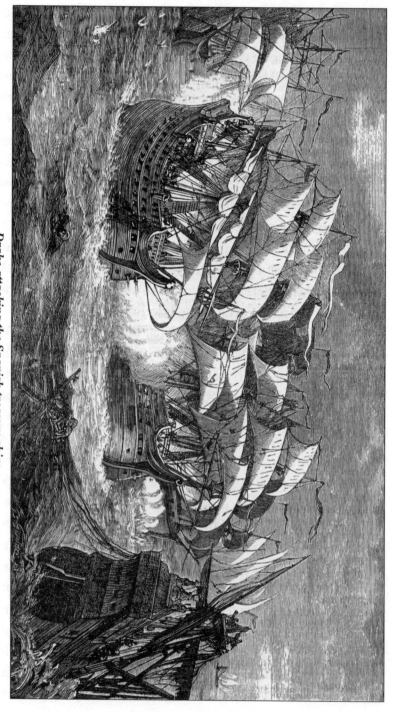

Drake attacking the Spanish treasure ships.

of the bedchamber, who (Welwood asserts in his memoirs) stole the keys from the pocket of the pontiff while he slept. Bishop Burnet observes that Walsingham's chief spies were priests, and he used to say "an active but vicious priest was the best spy in the world."

Drake sailed from the Thames, Strype says, with forty galleys, for the coast of Spain. Four of these were the largest ships of the queen; the remainder were furnished and equipped for him by the merchants of London, in hope of making profit out of the plunder. His chief ships were the *Bonaventure*; the *Lion* commanded by William Borough, Comptroller of the Navy; the *Dreadnought*, Captain Fenner: and the *Rainbow*, Captain Bellingham.

After anchoring in Plymouth Sound, he learned from two Dutch vessels which he hailed, that a Spanish fleet, richly laden, was lying at Cadiz, ready to sail for Lisbon, the rendezvous of the intended Armada. He bore boldly for that harbour. Six galleys which endeavoured to make head against him he compelled to run for shelter under cover of a fire from the forts. In spite of the latter, he plundered and sank or burned more than 100 vessels laden with provisions, arms, and ammunition. Among them were two stately galleons, one belonging to the Marquis of Santa Cruz, the other to the Venetians of Ragusa, mounting many brass cannon. Running thence along the coast to Cape St. Vincent, he stormed the castle on that promontory, and other fortresses, and pillaged the towns in succession, till he came to the mouth of the Tagus, when he in vain endeavoured to lure out the Marquis of Santa Cruz to fight him, by plundering and burning all the ships he found there.

Sailing thence to the Azores, he met on the way, near the isle of St. Michael, a mighty carack, called the *San Philipo*, returning from the East Indies, and captured her with ease; and the papers that were found on board of her so fully illustrated to the English the value of Indian merchandise, and the mode of trading in the Eastern Hemisphere, that "they afterwards," says Camden, "set up a gainful trade and traffic, establishing a company of East India merchants."

The loss of the provisions and stores which Drake destroyed at Cadiz, in what he jocularly termed "singeing the King of Spain's beard," compelled Philip to defer his darling project of invading England for another year, and gave that country time to prepare; while, by the success of the expeditions of Drake, her seamen were fast learning to despise the great and unwieldy ships of the Spaniards, who ere the year closed had fresh source for disgust, when Rear-Admiral Sir John Hawkins, when lying with a fleet of Her Majesty's ships in the Catwater, fired a shot into the Spanish admiral, who came into Plymouth with the fleet that was to escort Anne of Austria, for not striking his flag, "and paying the usual honours to Her Majesty's colours, which, after much altercation, he compelled him to do "("Lives of the Admirals "). And now came the year 1588, when Philip II hoped to have a sure and terrible vengeance for all the past.

- C H A P T E R   V I I I -

THE SPANISH ARMADA, 1588

UNDOUBTEDLY THE greatest event of Elizabeth's reign was the defeat of the Invincible Armada - the mighty fleet destined by Philip to conquer England. His grand or ostensible object was the destruction of Protestantism; but he was smarting under a consciousness of repeated insults, of territories ravaged, cities burned, and the loss of many great treasure-ships. His vanity was also wounded by Elizabeth's refusal to marry him, as her sister had done; and after the death of Mary Stuart, whose execution was deemed by all Europe an outrage on the law of nations, he did not conceal his claims to the double inheritance of the crowns of England and Scotland, which she had bequeathed to him from the scaffold at Fotheringay.

His ambassador, Mendoza, thus wrote to him: "God having been pleased to suffer this accursed nation to fall under His displeasure, not only in regard to spiritual affairs by heresy, but also in what relates to worldly affairs, by this terrible event (the death of Mary), it is plain that the Almighty has wished to give your Majesty these two crowns as your own entire possession."

John Leslie, the celebrated Bishop of Ross, and the devoted adherent of Mary, wrote in French and Latin and in English, a declaration to prove that Philip II was lawful heir to the throne of England, the King of Scotland having rendered himself incompetent to succeed, in consequence of his heresy from Rome. The Duke de Guise was of the same opinion, and consigned to the King of Spain the task of avenging Mary Stuart, and securing Catholicism in England; and having at his disposal the ships and seamen of all Spain, Portugal, and

Italy, with troops deemed then the finest in Europe, with all the treasures of the New World, he seemed to possess resources sufficient for the mighty enterprise he resolved to undertake - an enterprise which he had conceived so early as 1570, and began to execute in 1588.

The roadstead of Lisbon was to be the general muster-place of the fleet; and there, in the spring of 1588, assembled the shipping furnished by Sicily, Naples, Catalonia, Andalusia, Castile, and Biscay. These vessels were of various dimensions. There were caravels, caracks, xebecs, galleys (the general craft of the time), some with sails, some with oars; a number of galleons; and four galeases of enormous size, that towered like wooden citadels amid the lesser vessels of the fleet. Their forecastles were literally fortified, and carried several tiers of guns. This fleet had on board 21,556 troops, who were to land on the coast of England. They were carefully equipped with arms and ammunition of every kind, and had provisions sufficient for a six months'campaign in the field. The Vicar-General of the Holy Office was on board, with a hundred Jesuits and other priests, to work the re-conversion of the island; and while this vast armament was preparing at Lisbon, under the command of the Marquis de Santa Cruz, one of the most successful admirals of the age, the Duke of Parma was concentrating a vast force on the coast of Flanders to follow up the first blow, if successful. That able captain, besides his garrisons, received under his

Wrought-iron breech-loading ship gun, from the wreck of the "Mary Rose" (Tower Collection).

colours 5,000 men from Central Italy, 4,000 from Naples, 9,000 from Castile and Arragon, 3,000 from Germany, together with four squadrons of reiters; and he had 800 Englishmen under the deserter Sir William Stanley, with other forces from the Walloon country and from Franche Comte'. He felled the whole forest of Waes to build flat-bottomed boats for the conveyance of 100,000 horse and foot down the canals to Nieuport and Dunkirk for transport to the mouth of the Thames, under the escort of the mighty Armada.

All manner of machines used in sieges, and of material for building bridges, forming camps, and building fortresses, fascines, field and garrison gun-carriages, were also prepared at a vast expenditure of money and labour; and Pope Sixtus had pledged himself to advance a million of ducats the moment the expedition touched the soil of England. In a bull intended to be secret until the hour of landing, the anathema hurled against Elizabeth by Pius V and Gregory XIII, as a bastard and heretic, deposed her from the throne. Nor did the scheme end there, for it was confidently expected that the Most Catholic King, who already possessed the Netherlands, Spain, Portugal, the Indies, and nearly all Italy, on making himself master of England on one hand, and on the other of Scotland, would turn the arms of them all against Constantinople, and expel the Turks from Europe. A letter of Sir John Hawkins to Sir Francis Walsingham computes the Armada at 114 vessels; but the Spanish historians affirm it to have amounted to 132 sail, divided into squadrons (See table on following page).

This number is exclusive of 2,088 galley-slaves. On board the fleet was a vast quantity of military stores for the land service, consisting of single and double cannon, culverins, and field-pieces, 7,000 muskets, 10,000 halberds, 56,000 quintals of gunpowder, and 12,000 quintals of match. Moreover, the ships were laden with horses, mules, carts, wheels, wagons, spades, and mattocks, and all things requisite for a permanent residence in England. An enormous quantity of saddles and bridles were provided. At Dunkirk 20,000 empty casks were collected, with ropes to make floating bridges; and to the conquest of England, as in the days of Harold the Saxon, there came nobles and princes from many places, crowding under the banner of Alonzo Perez de Gusman, the Duke of Medina Sidonia, who had succeeded the Marquis de Santa Cruz in the command, for which he was quite unqualified; but he had two able seconds in Juan Manez de Recaldez, of Biscay, and Miguel de Orquendo, of Guipuzcoa. Among these were the Duke of Petrana, from Spain, the Marquis de Bourgou, son of the Archduke Ferdinand of Austria, Vespasian di Gonzaga, of the house of Mantua, a great soldier, who had once been Viceroy of Spain; Giovanni di

	Ships	Tons	Guns	Sailors	Soldiers
The Portuguese Galleons, under the Generalissimo	12	7,739	389	1,242	3,086
Biscayan Squadron, under Don Juan Manez de Recaldez, Captain-General	14	5,681	302	906	2,117
Castilian Squadron, under Don Diego de Valdez	16	8,054	477	1,793	2,624
Andalusian Squadron, under Don Pedro de Valdez	11	8,692	315	776	2,359
Guipuzcoan Squadron	14	7,192	296	608	2,120
Levant Squadron, under Don Martin Vertondonna	10	8,632	319	844	2,793
Squadron of Hulks, under Don Juan Lopez de Medina	23	10,860	446	950	4,170
Squadron of Xebecs, &c., under Don Antonio Mendoza	24	2,090	204	746	1,103
Galeases of Naples, under Don Hugo de Monendo	4	-	200	477	744
Galleys of Portugal, under Don Diego de Medina	4	-	200	424	440
Total	132	58,940	3,148	8,766	21,556

The squadrons on the Armada according to Spanish historians.

Medici, the Bastard of Florence; Amadeo of Savoy, and many others.

Meanwhile the Queen of England and her people were not idle in preparing to resist this mighty armament, the fame of which filled all Europe. Elizabeth summoned her most- able councillors, some of whom, like Raleigh, Grey, Bingham, Norris, and Grenville, had been bred to arms, and possessed military talents of a very high order.

It was resolved to equip a fleet adequate to the great emergency, and to raise all the land forces possible; and for this purpose circular letters were addressed to the lords-lieutenants of the different counties, and the returns showed that there could be raised for the defence of England 132,689 men, of whom 14,000 were cavalry. These levies were exclusive of the city of London, which offered the queen 10,000 men and 30 ships; and, as Stow records, "The merchants met every Tuesday to practise all points of war. Some of them, in 1588, had charge of men in the great camp, and were called Captains of the Artillery Garden." Their first place of meeting was in Tasel Close, now Artillery Lane, Bishopsgate.

Along the southern coast were disposed 20,000 men j under the Earl of Hunsdon, 45,000 men were collected for the special defence of the queen's person; 1,000 horse and 22,000 foot were posted at Tilbury, to protect London against the Prince of Parma; and, as Macaulay's noble ballad has it -

"From Eddystone to Berwick bounds, from Lynn to Milford Bay,

The time of slumber was as bright and busy as the day."

In Scotland, the king, who had rejected the proposals of the Spaniards to ally themselves with him, and to invade England by the borders with an army under Parma, took all the necessary measures for defence, by the erection of beacons, and the enrolment of every man above sixteen years of age, capable of bearing arms, in the kingdom; on which Elizabeth sent Sir Robert Sidney as a special ambassador to thank him, and promise assistance if the Spanish troops landed on the Scottish shores. On the 4th of August, he wrote to Elizabeth from Edinburgh, to the effect that he did not propose to aid the English as a foreign prince, but as their countryman and her "natural-born son" (Rymer).

The ships of the English navy at this time amounted only to thirty-six; but the largest and most serviceable of the merchant vessels were collected from various ports to form a fleet, to man which there came forward 17,472 mariners. The number of ships was 191; their total tonnage was only 31,985; but there was one, the *Triumph*, of 1,100 tons, one of 1,000, one of 900, others smaller, and twenty of only 200 tons. Assistance was given by the Dutch, who sent, as Stow has it, "threescore sail, brave ships of war, fierce, and full of spleen, not so much for England's aid as in just occasion for their own defence."

The command of the fleet was given to Lord Howard of Effingham, High Admiral of England, and his vice-admirals were Sir Francis Drake, Sir John Hawkins, and Sir Martin Frobisher, men whose names, even after the lapse of nearly three centuries, are still their country's pride.

On the 12th of July the Armada put finally to sea; the orders of Philip to the Duke de Medina Sidonia being that "he should, on entering the Channel, keep near the French coast, and if attacked by the English ships, avoid an action, and steer on Calais Roads, where the Prince of Parma's squadron was to job him." As these many vessels spread their canvas to the breeze, the grandeur of the spectacle excited the most flattering anticipations of success, and thousands of hearts beat high with the hope of conquest and visions of coming glory.

But the duke having been informed that the English fleet were lying "off their guard," in Plymouth Sound, could not resist the chance of destroying it there; and, deviating from his orders, he stood at once across to the coast of England. On the 19th of July the Armada was off the Lizard, where a Scottish privateer's-man, Captain Thomas Fleming, saw them, and hoisting every inch of canvas, ran into Plymouth to warn the English admiral. By sound of cannon and trumpet the crews were summoned on board; and though a stiff south-west wind was blowing, the, vessels worked out into the offing. Lord Howard that night got clear out to sea with only six of his ships, but between twenty and thirty more came out in the morning; and with these under easy sail, he stood along shore in view of the cliffs they had come to defend, anxiously looking out for this long expected and terrible Armada,

"On the night of that memorable 19th of July, messengers and signals were dispatched fast and far through England to warn each town and village that the enemy had come at last! In every shire and every city there was instant mustering of horse and man; in every seaport there was instant making ready for sea; and, especially along the southern coast, there was hurrying to join the Admiral of England, and to share in the honour of the first encounter with the foe "(Creasy). Among those who came thus with their ships were the Earls of Oxford, Northumberland, and Cumberland, Sir Robert and Sir Thomas Cecil, Sir Walter Raleigh, Sir Thomas Gerard, and others. "Upon the newes being sent to Court from Plymouth of their certain arrival," says Robert, Earl of Monmouth, in his "Personal Memoirs," "my Lord Cumberland and myselfe tooke post-horses and rode straight to Portsmouth, where we found a frigate that carried us to sea."

With a fleet amounting ultimately to 140 ships, when near the rock known as the Eddystone, the admiral discovered the Armada to the westward as far as Fowey, sailing in the form of a half-moon, seven miles in length. All were under full sail, yet coming slowly up the Channel. "The ships appeared like so

99

many floating castles," says Lediard, in his old "Naval History," "and the ocean seemed to groan under the weight of their heavy burdens. The Lord High Admiral willingly suffered them to pass by him, so that he might chase them in the rear, with all the advantage of the wind;" in other words, he got the weather-gage of the Duke of Medina Sidonia.

The two fleets were sailing thus on the morning of Sunday, the 21st July, when, six miles westward of the Eddystone, Lord Howard, at nine o'clock, sent forward a pinnace named the *Defiance*, "to denounce war," by a discharge of all her guns - a demonstration which he immediately seconded by the fire of his own ship, the *Ark Royal*, which opened a furious cannonade on the ship of Don Alphonso de Leva, which from its size he

Sir Francis Drake.

supposed to be that of the Spanish admiral. Shortening sail, he poured a terrible fire into her, and would have destroyed her had she not been rescued by several other vessels closing in.

Now Drake, Hawkins, and Frobisher vigorously engaged the enemy's sternmost ship, under the Captain-General, Don Juan, the Marquis de Recaldez, who was on board one of the Portuguese galleons, and did all that a brave man could do to keep his squadron together; but, in spite of all his efforts, so sternly was he attacked, that they were given among the main body of the fleet, while his own vessel was so battered in the hull by shot that she became quite unserviceable.

The Spanish fleet being somewhat scattered now, the Duke of Medina Sidonia signalled for the ships to close, and, hoisting more sail, sought to hold on his course towards Calais; and now the battle took the form of a running fight.

In this movement a great galleon, commanded by Don Pedro Valdez, being seriously battered in her hull and wrecked aloft, fell foul of another ship, and was so disabled that she was left astern by the rest, just as night was coming on, and the sea running high; and the English admiral, supposing that she had neither soldiers nor sailors on board, passed her in the pursuit. On the morning of the 22nd, she was seen by Sir Francis Drake, who sent a pinnace with orders for her to surrender; but Don Pedro Valdez replied, "I have 450 men on board, and stand too much upon my honour to yield."

He then propounded certain conditions; to which the response of the vice-admiral was that "he might yield or not, as he chose, but he should soon find that Drake was no coward."

Don Pedro, on learning that his immediate opponent was Drake, whose name was a terror to the Spaniards, yielded at once, and his ship was sent into Plymouth. Prior to this, Drake divided among his own crew 55,000 golden ducats which he found on board of her.

On the same night that Don Pedro was abandoned, the Spaniards had another mishap. A great ship, of Biscay, commanded by Don Miguel de Orquendo, was maliciously set on fire by a Dutch gunner, whom he had ill used; but other ships closed in, and the crews extinguished the flames, yet not until her upper deck was blown off. "Drake had been ordered to carry lights that night," records Lediard; "but being in full chase of five German hulks, or merchant ships, which he supposed to be the enemy's, happened to neglect it. This was the cause that most of the fleet lay by (to?) all night, because they could not see the lights."

That night the Spanish fleet bore on by the Start, and next morning they were seen far to the leeward; and Sir Francis Drake, with his ships, did not rejoin the admiral until evening, as he had pursued the enemy within "culverin-shot" till daybreak.

The whole of this day was spent by the duke in repairing damages, and putting his fleet in order. He commanded Don Alphonso de Leva to bring the first and last squadrons together; assigning to each ship its station in battle, according to a plan agreed upon in Spain, and any deviation from which involved the penalty of death. Orquendo's great ship had her crew and valuables taken out of her, and was cast adrift. She was found by Captain John Hawkins, with "fifty poor wretches" on board, the stench of whose half-burned bodies was horrible. A prize-crew took her into Weymouth,

After a calm night - the wind being northerly - on the following morning the Spaniards tacked, and bore down upon the English; who also tacked, and stood westward. After several attempts to gain the weather-gage, another battle ensued, which was marked only by confusion and variety of success. The English ships, being better handled and lighter in draught than the unwieldy argosies of the Spaniards, stood quickly off or on, as their captains saw fit, The firing was now ringing over the Channel for many miles; and while, in one quarter, some ships of London which were completely surrounded by the Spaniards were gallantly rescued, in another, the latter, with equal bravery, saved from capture their Admiral Recaldez." The great guns on both sides rattled like so many peals of thunder; but the shot from the high-built Spanish ships flew for the most part over the heads of the English, without doing much execution."

A Mr. Cock, who was gallantly fighting a little volunteer ship of his own, named the *Delight*, was the only Englishman of note killed. Some officers advised Lord Howard to grapple and board; but knowing that the Spaniards had 20,000 soldiers on board, he wisely declined to do so, as loss on his side would peril

Blade of the sword of Sir Francis Drake
(Sir Sibbald Scott's "British Army").

the safety of all England. The Spaniards at first bore down under a press of sail, as if they meant to board the English; but seeing that the *Ark*, the *Nonpareil*, the *Elizabeth Jonas*, the *Victory*, and others, were prepared to meet them, they were content to drop astern of the second-named ship.

In the meantime, the *Triumph*, *Merchant-Royal*, *Centurion*, *Margaret*, *John*, *Mary Rose*, and *Golden Lion*, being far to leeward, and separated from the rest of the fleet, were borne down upon by the great gal-eases of Naples, and a fierce conflict ensued for an hour and a half, till the Neapolitans sheered off, when a change of wind to the south west enabled a squadron of English ships to attack the western flank of the Spanish fleet with such fury that they were all compelled to give way; and so, till the sun began to set, the desultory and running fight went on. Wherever the firing was hottest, Lord Howard's ship was seen. In this day's strife a great ship of Venice and many smaller were taken; and the *Mayflower*, a merchantman of London, behaved bravely, "like a man-of-war."

On the 24th of July there was a cessation of hostilities on both sides, and Lord Howard, being short of ammunition, sent the pinnaces inshore for a supply of powder and ball, as both had failed in the fleet. Sir Walter Raleigh, in recording this great mistake, says "that many of our great guns stood but as ciphers and scarecrows, not unlike to the Easterling hulks, who were wont to paint great red port-holes in their broadsides, where they carried no ordnance at all."

On the 25th, the *St. Anne*, a great Portuguese galleon, was taken near the Isle of Wight by Captain John Hawkins, under the fire of the Spaniards, who attempted to rescue her. On this clay, the further to encourage his gallant captains, the Lord Admiral knighted the Lords Howard and Sheffield, Roger Townsend, John Hawkins, Martin Frobisher, and others; and it was resolved not to assail the enemy any more until they came into the narrower part of the Channel, between Dover and Calais, before which last-named place the Armada came to anchor on the 27th of July, and the Duke of Medina Sidonia in vain dispatched a second urgent message to the Duke of Parma for aid.

On the 28th the Lord Admiral resorted to a means of destruction hitherto totally unknown in naval warfare - fire-ships. Selecting eight of the worst craft in his fleet, he bestowed on them plenty of pitch, tar, resin, brimstone, and everything that was inflammable. Their cannon he had loaded with bullets, chains, iron bars, and other missiles of destruction. Thus equipped, with all their canvas set, he sent them before the wind and with the tide, about two hours before midnight, under the command of two captains named Prowse and Young, right into the heart of the Spanish fleet. On coming within a certain distance, they lashed the helms, set fire to the trains, dropped into their boats, and withdrew.

Their approach was no sooner discovered by the Spaniards, as they came with their hulls, masts, and rigging all sheeted with fire, than the utmost consternation ensued. "Many of them had been at the siege of Antwerp, and had seen the destructive machines made use of there. Suspecting, therefore, that these were big with such-like engines, they set up a most hideous clamour of 'Cut your cables ! Get up your anchors !'and immediately, in a panic, put to sea."

All was now confusion and precipitation, and another large galleon, having had her rudder unshipped, was tossed about till she was stranded on the sands of Calais, where she was taken by Sir Amyas Preston, in the admiral's long-boat, accompanied by other boats manned by 100 seamen. Her flag was not hauled down without a bloody scuffle, in which her captain, Don Hugo de Moncada, was shot through the head, and 400 of her soldiers and rowers drowned or put to the sword. After 303 galley-slaves and 50,000 ducats had been taken out of her, she was abandoned as a wreck to Gordon, the Governor of Calais.

After the terror, flight, and miserable disasters by which many of their ships were driven into the North Sea, and others on the Flemish coast, the Spaniards, ranging themselves in the best order they could, approached Gravelines; but, as the English had got the weather-gage, they could obtain supplies neither there nor at Dunkirk. In the meantime, Sir Francis Drake, in the *Revenge*, Sir John Hawkins, in the *Victory*, Captain Fenner, in the *Nonpareil*, Sir George Beeston, in the *Dreadnought*, Sir Robert Southwell, in the *Elizabeth Jonas*, and other brave officers, kept pouring in their shot upon them continually, "and tore many of their ships so dreadfully that the water entered on all sides; and some, flying for relief towards Ostend, were shot through and through again by the Zealanders." In this day's action, a great galleon was so mauled by the *Bonaventure*, *Rainbow*, and *Vanguard*, that she sank, like a stone, in the night. Then a great galleon of Biscay, with two other vessels, was sunk.

The galleon *St. Matthew*, under Don Diego de Pimentelli, coming to the aid of Don Francisco de Toledo (colonel of thirty-two companies), in the *St. Philip*, which had been terribly cut up by the ships of Lord Henry Seymour and Sir William Winter, was taken by the Dutch; while the *St. Philip*, after being pursued as far as Ostend, was captured by some ships of Flushing. The Spaniards were now fighting simply to escape.

On the 31st of July the wind was blowing hard in the morning, from the north-west, and on the Spaniards making a last desperate attempt to recover the Channel again, were driven towards Zealand; upon which the English, who had followed them so closely for so many days, gave over the chase, supposing the Great Armada to be utterly ruined, and in danger of running aground upon the shoals and shallows of that flat and sandy coast.

The Duke of Medina Sidonia now held a Council of War, at which it was unanimously resolved, as it was impossible to repass the English Channel; as they were in want of many things, especially cannon-shot; as their ships were miserably battered and torn; as their anchors had been slipped in Calais Roads; as provisions were short, and water was spent; as many had been slain, and many were sick and wounded; and as there was no hope now of their being joined by the Duke of Parma, whose armament was blockaded by the Hollanders, they should return to Spain north-about by the coast of Scotland.

To save water, all the cavalry horses and baggage mules were flung overboard, and all sail was made for the North Sea. Leaving a squadron, under Lord Henry Seymour, to assist the Dutch in blocking up the Prince of Parma, and sending another, under Sir William Winter, to guard the coast, the Lord Admiral with the main body of his victorious fleet pursued the flying foe as far as the Firth of Forth. He confidently believed it was the duke's design to put in there, and he had taken measures for his utter destruction; but finding that the Spaniards bore on their course to the north, he relinquished the pursuit.

Most miserable was the future fate of the Armada. Of the duke's vessels, many were cast away among the Scottish isles, and seventeen, with 5,394 men on board, on the coast of Ireland; among others, a stately galleon and two Venetian ships of great burden. All who were shipwrecked in Ireland were put to the sword, or perished by the hands of the common executioner; the Lord-Deputy, by whose barbarous orders this was done, excusing himself on pretence that they might join the rebels. Thirty-eight ships, that were driven by a strong west wind into the Channel, were there taken by the English, and others by the Rochellers, in France.

The chief treasure-ship, it was long alleged, was plundered and blown up by Macleod of Dunvegan, in the west of Scotland;

and towards the close of the last century a frigate was sent by the Spanish Government to investigate the story and the locality. Whether the crew found any treasure in the bay is unknown; but, from the circumstance of their mutinying and becoming pirates, it was currently supposed they had done so. A cannon from this or one of the other wrecks of the Armada is now in the castle of Inverary. Macleod is said to have used her artillery and soldiers successfully in the furtherance of a feud with one of his neighbours.

In the treatment of those unfortunate castaways, Scotland, though sternly Presbyterian, was very unlike Catholic Ireland. There was one incident occurred at this period which, though it had little to do with the great events we have narrated, has been deemed worthy of a place-in history, inasmuch as it shows that the detestation of Catholicism, rendered more keen by the recent warlike attempt to subvert the Protestant institutions of both kingdoms, did not in any degree repress the promptings of humanity towards Catholic people in distress.

Early one morning, many days before the fate of the Armada was known in Scotland, one of the Spanish ships, having on board 700 men, was thrown ashore by a tempest near the little seaport of Anstruther, on the coast of Fife; but so far were the inhabitants from taking this opportunity of imprisoning or otherwise punishing their enemies, who were now completely at their mercy, that they supplied the Spanish soldiers and seamen with clothing, food, and shelter, while the commander (who was an admiral) and his officers were kept by a gentleman at his house until they obtained the king's permission to depart home. Thus far Melvil tells us in his Diary; and Lediard adds that they were sent by James VI. to the Duke of Parma, in the Netherlands; a third authority has it, after a year's detention in Scotland- For three successive Sundays the Scots celebrated the victory of the English.

Of all the ships that sailed from Lisbon, only fifty-three returned to Spain; of the four galeases of Naples, but one; of the four galleons of Portugal, but one; of the ninety-one great hulks from many provinces, there returned only thirty, fifty-eight being lost. In short, Philip lost in this expedition eighty-one ships, 3,500 soldiers, above 2,000 prisoners in England and in the Low Countries; and, to conclude, there was no noble or honourable family in all the Spanish peninsula but had to mourn for a son, a brother, or a dear kinsmar, who had found his grave in the Channel, on the shores of Ireland, or amid the bleak rocky isles of Western Scotland. Distressed, tossed, and wasted by storms and miseries, the remnant came home about the end of September, only to encounter sorrow, shame, and dishonour.

Camden says that Philip received the news of the ill-success of his fleet with heroic patience; and that when he heard of its total defeat, he thanked God it was no worse. But, according to Anthony Coppley, an English fugitive, who was present, Philip was at mass when the tidings came, and at its conclusion "he swore that he would waste and consume his crown, even to the value of a candlestick (pointing to one that stood upon the altar) but either he would utterly ruin Her Majesty and England or else himself, and let Spain become tributary to her."

The Duke of Medina Sidonia was forbidden to appear at Court. His title was taken from a small city in Eastern Andalusia, which was made, in 1445, a duchy for the powerful family of Gusman, of which there were three other dukes and two marquises. The Spanish priests, who had so frequently blessed the Armada and foretold its success, were puzzled for a time to account discovered that all the calamities of Spain were caused by their permitting the infidel Moors to linger so long in Granada.

Meantime, England resounded with acclamation and rejoicing. Eleven standards taken from the enemy were hung

Vessels of the Armada wrecked on the Irish coast.

in St. Paul's Cathedral, whither Elizabeth went in procession from her palace at Whitehall to a public thanksgiving, on the 24th of November. She proceeded through the then quaint and gable-ended streets of Old London, in a triumphal chariot with four pillars; two supporting an imperial crown, the other two the lion of England and the dragon of Wales, with the royal arms between them.

It is from the portrait of Elizabeth taken in the dress she wore on this great occasion, that we are so familiar with the extravagant style of costume she adopted. It was engraved by Crispin de Passe, from a drawing by Isaac Oliver. She prayed audibly on her knees at the west door of St. Paul's.

Several medals were struck in England in honour of this victory. One, in honour of the queen, represented the fire-ships and fleet in hurry and confusion, with the inscription, *"Dux Fcemina Facti."* Another was struck in honour of the English navy. "It was, ''says Sir William Monson, a brave and pious old English seaman, and one of Elizabeth's most able commanders, "the will of Him that directs all men and their actions, that the fleets should meet and the enemy be beaten as they were; that they should be put from their anchorage in Calais Roads while the Prince of Parma was beleaguered at sea, and their navy driven about Scotland and Ireland with great hazard and loss, which showeth how God did marvellously defend us against their dangerous designs. By this, too, we may learn how weak and feeble are the schemes of men in respect of the Creator of man; and how impartially He dealt between the two nations, sometimes giving to the one, sometimes to the other, the advantage, yet so that He alone super-eminently ordered the battle."

- C H A P T E R   I X -
THE GROYNE, 1589

THE TOTAL defeat of the Armada had inspired the nation with an enthusiastic passion for enterprises against the Spaniards by land and sea, and nothing now seemed impossible to the English sailor or soldier. It happened in 1589, that is to say in the year subsequent to the Armada, that Don Antonio, Prior of Crato, and Knight of Malta, a natural son of one of the royal family of Portugal (the throne of which Philip I. of Spain had seized in right of his wife, Donna Maria, daughter of John III), trusting to the aversion of his countrymen to the Castilians, who tyrannised over them and treated them with contempt, had advanced a claim to the crown; and visiting first France and then England, found both Henry and Elizabeth willing to favour his pretensions, the further to humble Philip II.

A scheme was formed by the people, rather than the Government, of England, to conquer or wrest the kingdom of Portugal from Spain for Don Antonio; and the leaders of this romantic enterprise were Sir Francis Drake and Sir John Norris.

Twenty thousand men volunteered to serve on this expedition, and of these 4,000 were seamen. Resolving to act with prudence and economy, the queen gave them only six ships of war and 6,000 men. The following are the names of the ships and the commanders, as given by Sir William Monson:- *Revenge*, Sir Francis Drake; *Dreadnought*, Captain Thomas Fenner; *Aid*, Captain William Fenner; *Nonpareil*, Captain William Sackville; *Foresight*, Captain Sir William Winter; *Swiftsure*, Captain Sir William Goring.

The leaders of the land forces under Norris were - his kinsmen, Sir Edward and Sir Henry Norris, Sir Roger Williams, and Captain Williams (or Wilson), sergeant-major.

On the 18th of April, 1589, they sailed from Plymouth, having with them the Prior of Crato, whom they styled King of Portugal. The Dutch added some ships to the expedition, and these, with the queen's and others hired by the leaders, made up altogether eighty sail, according to one authority - 146 according to another - but the circumstance of Robert d'Evereaux, the Earl of Essex, K.G., joining them at sea, with certain ships which he had also hired, makes some confusion as to the exact number. With- the earl came his brother, Walter, Sir Roger Williams, Sir Philip Butler, and Sir Edward Wingfield.

A few days later saw them all off the bay of the Groyne, and menacing the Galician town of Betanzos, which is situated on the declivity of a hill washed on the east and west by the river Mandes, and four leagues south-west of La Corunna.

It is supposed that had they sailed direct to Portugal, the good-will of the people might have ensured them success; but hearing of preparations that were making at the Groyne for another invasion of England, they were induced to go thither and destroy this new armament of Spain.

This expedition was full of the elements of weakness. A number of wild spirits were collected together without discipline, and crowded in small ships, without surgeons, or carriage for sick or wounded men in case of casualties, and without sufficient provisions. Hence, we are told, in the Appendix to the "Spanish Invasion," there was much quarrelling and much drunkenness. In many of its features the enterprise somewhat resembled the British auxiliary Spanish Legion, under General Evans, in more recent times, which was partly countenanced and partly repudiated by the Whig Government, with trickery and policy.

The first landing was effected in a bay more than an English mile distant from the Groyne, by boats and pinnaces; this was accomplished without opposition, as no such invasion was expected. The force, whose strength is not stated, consisting of pikemen and musketeers, with some small pieces of artillery, advanced at once against Betanzos, within half a mile of which they encountered some Spanish troops sent forward by Don Juan de Luna, the governor. These they charged, routed, and drove within the gates. For that night they occupied the villages, mills, and other buildings around the town of Betanzos, while the Spanish fleet cannonaded them from the roadstead, filling the unfortunate Spaniards with alarm and perplexity, as many shot fell among them.

Next morning, Sir John Norris having landed some more artillery, the first shot he fired had the effect of sending the shipping out of the roadstead; and even a great galleon that lay amid them, a remnant of the last year's Armada, ceased to fire on them, though commanded by Don Juan Manez de Recaldez, Vice-Admiral of Spain. The assault of the lower town was now resolved on, and for that purpose, 200 men were landed in boats and pinnaces, the guns of which played upon it as they approached; while on the land side 500 men were to enter at low water, if the way proved passable, and 300 were to storm the walls by escalade at another point.

A few men were wounded as the boats came in shore, but in a few minutes the lower town of Betanzos was entered at three points; all who resisted were put to the sword. Thus 500 were slain in the streets. Abandoning their goods, the inhabitants fled to the upper town, to the rocks, or hid themselves in cellars and *bodegas*. A few surrendered; among others, the governor, Don Juan de Luna, and a commissary, from whom they learned that 500 of the soldiers in garrison had been in the Armada, and that there were vast stores for the new-projected expedition to England. These were all destroyed; and the soldiers, finding the cellars full of wine, indulged themselves in such excessive drinking - using even their helmets as goblets - that many of them fell sick and died.

The Spaniards seem to have acted with much pusillanimity. They now set fire to the great galleon, and such was her size that she was two days and a night in burning. Before firing her, they so overloaded her cannon that thirty-four of them burst, with a succession of mighty crashes, sending showers of burning brands over all then-other shipping, which they abandoned to the foe, who now attacked the other, or upper town, which was steeply situated, and very difficult of access. The walls were undermined, the mines sprung, and two breaches made, one of them partially in a large tower.

The stormers went bravely in with sword and pike, but the shattered tower gave way in the very midst of them, and buried about thirty under masses of masonry. The dust, the noise, and the suddenness of the catastrophe "so amazed the rest that they forsook their commanders," and, in retiring through a narrow lane, great numbers of them were shot down by the garrison.

A breach made by the cannon, "though it was well assaulted by our men," says the old folio account, "who came to push of pike at the top, and were ready to enter, yet the loose earth slipping outwards, by reason of their weight, half the wall remained entire, and so nothing was done, because our culverin and demi-culverin - we had but three pieces - were not sufficient to batter a defensible rampart."

A cloister, however, was stormed ere they fell back; and during these operations a colonel, named Huntley, with one detachment, and Captain Anthony Sampson with another, ravaged all the adjacent country, and brought into camp many cattle and sheep. On the day after the assault failed, Sir John Norris learned from a prisoner that the Conde de Andrada, at the head of 8,000 Spaniards, was advancing from Puente de Burgos to the relief of Betanzos, after forming a junction with a much larger force, under the Conde de Altamira.

On the 6th of May he marched to meet Andrada with

nine English regiments (for that military term was now fully determined and understood), leaving five with Sir Francis Drake to guard the artillery and cover the cloister. Norris moved in three columns, and a march of six miles brought him to Puente de Burgos, where he found the conde's troops under arms to receive him.

They were charged by the first column, under Captain Middleton, who was so well supported by the second, under Captain Wingfield, that they were "beaten from place to place," till they retired in confusion over a stone bridge that crossed a creek of the sea, and into their camp, which lay beyond it, and was strongly entrenched; and as they retired they left a guard at the bridge, which was heavily barricaded with barrels. But, on seeing Sir Edward Norris, at the head of his pikemen, with Colonel Sidney, and Captains Hinder, Fulford, and Barton, coming resolutely on, the barricade was abandoned, and the bridge crossed. The entrenched camp was then entered, sword in hand, Sir Edward leading the way, till he was severely wounded by a rapier. After a very short conflict, the Spaniards were routed, driven out, and put to flight.

Their royal standard, with the arms of Castile and Leon upon it, was taken, and for three miles bodies of the fugitives were pursued by the victorious English, who slew vast numbers of them among hedges and vineyards. "They put 200 to death in a cloister: and all this with the loss of only one captain and one man killed, and a few wounded."

The country was then ravaged, and for more than three miles in extent was all red flame and dusky smoke. On returning, they reshipped their artillery, with all that was found in the Groyne, set fire to the lower town and the monastery, embarked the troops on the 8th, and sailed, leaving the shore black with smoking ruins, and the bay strewed with the burned wrecks of those ships which were to have been another Armada.

This landing at the Groyne was quite a deviation from the original plan; but now, after sailing along the coast, they arrived, on the 16th, at Peniche, a fortified town of Portugal, in the province of Estra-madura. Its position is still a strong one; the fortress there had been recently erected by Philip II., and the harbour, though small, afforded the safest anchorage.

Sir John Norris now landed with the infantry, and the castle was surrendered without a shot being fired, to the Prior of Crato, as Don Antonio, King of Portugal, at whose earnest persuasion an instant march to Lisbon was resolved on. Prior to the surrender of the castle, five companies of Spaniards made a sally from the town, but were charged and routed by two of English, under the Earl of Essex. After taking from the castle 100 pikes and muskets, and twenty barrels of powder, the daring march for Lisbon began, under Sir John Norris; while Sir Francis Drake was to take up the fleet by the river Tagus, but failed to do so. The first night's halt was at Lorinha; and a twelve miles' farther march brought them next day to the now famous ground of Torres Vedras, the strong castle of which they captured. This edifice was formerly the dower-house of the Queens of Portugal.

The third day's march saw some encounters with cavalry, a few Englishmen having been mounted to serve as such, under Captain Yorke. The latter, at the head of only forty of these new troopers, charged and broke through 200 Spanish horse in half-mail; and one of his corporals, with only eight, routed nearly forty more. That night, the regiment called "General Drake's" when halted at a hill near Lores, was set upon by treachery. A body of Spanish troops advanced and as they shouted "Viva el Rey Don Antonio!" were permitted to pass the guards, whom they instantly massacred but were speedily driven off by the main body. The 25th of May brought them to St. Katherine, one of the suburbs of Lisbon, the streets of which were scoured by Captain

Wingfield, at the head of a party of musketeers, who "met none but old folks and beggars, crying up the new king."That night the guards were properly posted, and the main body remained under arms all night, in a field near Alcantara, surrounded by groves of orange and lemon trees. There, weary with their long march and the weight of their arms, and wasted by lack of food, the inevitable complaint of all Peninsulai soldiering, many fell asleep, and while in this state a sortie was made upon them by the Spanish garrison in Lisbon. Colonel Bret and two captains, who endeavoured to make head against them, were slain, with many mere; but ere day broke they were repulsed by the Earl of Essex, who pursued them with sword and pike to the gates of the city, and even into the houses, where many of them were followed and killed by the English; and for every one of the latter who fell there perished more than three Spaniards.

During the march of Norris, Drake had been sailing by the Tagus, and had captured the town of Cascaes, on a promontory at the mouth of the river. The people fled thence into the high

Lisbon, from the sea.

rocky mountains of Cintra; but by a messenger he prevailed upon them to return and accept the Prior of Crato as their king.

General Norris now held a Council of War, as the position of his little force was very critical; and the question was whether he should await those Portuguese whom Don Antonio had asserted would flock to his standard, or begin a retreat at once. The opinions of his officers were so various that Norris had to act for himself; and after staying two nights in Lisbon, on finding that, of all his promised cavalry, Antonio could not muster a troop of horse, and, of all his infantry, barely two companies, though he had assured him "that upon his first landing there should be a revolt of all his subjects,"the English leader proposed to retire.

In the castle of Lisbon, then a strong edifice on the highest of the seven hills on which Lisbon stands, there was a garrison too numerous for him to attack with success, especially as he had very light artillery, so the" retreat began in the night. "Had we marched through his country as enemies," says the old narrator before quoted, "our army had been well supplied with all sorts of provisions; or had we plundered the suburbs of Lisbon, we had made ourselves the richest army that ever came out of England: for, besides the wealth of private dwellings, there were many great warehouses by the waterside full of all sorts of rich merchandise, but we were restrained from both of these." Don Antonio insisted on his subjects, as he called them, being spared, so the English gained little by their landing, and lost much. As they marched along the banks of the Tagus, in sight of the bare, sharp granite summits of Cintra, they were followed by the *adelantado* with the Spanish galleys, whose gunners fired on every opportunity, while their rear was galled by Spanish cavalry, who cut off those sick and wounded who fell in hundreds by the wayside, and for whom there were no means of conveyance.

At last they reached the castle of Cascaes, where a friar

informed them that a Spanish force was at hand, and had come as far as San Julian, a strong fort seven miles from Lisbon. This news was welcomed by the leaders, who were highly exasperated by the turn their affairs had taken, and promised the friar 100 crowns if his news proved true. The further to provoke an issue, the Earl of Essex sent a cartel to the Spanish general, offering to fight him singly, with ten men a side, or any equal number he chose.; and thereupon he marched next day to where the Spaniards had encamped, but found that they had made a precipitate retreat to Lisbon, and had, moreover, threatened to hang the English trumpeter who had brought the gallant earl's message.

After six cannon-shots had been discharged at Cascaes, the governor capitulated, and was permitted to march off with baggage and arms, but his cannon were taken. In fact, since the terrible issue of the Armada, the spirit of the Spaniards seemed to have fled; but Admiral Drake now rather lawlessly seized sixty large ships that belonged to the free Hans Cities, and were laden with goods for Lisbon, on the allegation that their cargoes were to have equipped the new Armada against England. On board of these he put troops, and the horses Norris had seized; and now the whole expedition put to sea, repulsing an attack made upon it by twenty great galleys of the enemy.

Still loth to leave Spain, they landed at Vigo, in Galicia, and burned the city, and ravaged all the adjacent country for eight miles inland. In the capture of Vigo, the timidity of the Spaniards was painfully apparent. Though every street in the city was strongly and peculiarly barricaded, on the appearance of 2,000 English, under Drake and Captain Wingfield, the whole garrison, save one man, fled to Bayonne ! After this Admiral Drake put to sea with twenty of the best ships, in hopes to overhaul the Spanish Indian fleet, while Sir John Norris and the Earl of Essex returned to England with the rest of this expedition, which proved a great source of mortification to the Spaniards, and raised still higher the warlike glory of the English; but it cost the lives of half of those who sailed, by sickness, famine, fatigue, and the sword. Of 1,100 gentlemen who embarked to serve as volunteers, only 350 survived when the fleet returned in the beginning of July; but Camden says they brought home 150 pieces of cannon and a great booty.

After enumerating the many causes which led to the failure of the expedition, Sir William Morison adds, in his "Reflections "upon it, that the want of field-pieces "was the loss of Lisbon; for its strength consisting in the castle, and we having only an army to countenance us, but no means for battery, we were the loss of the victory to ourselves; for it is apparent, by intelligence we received, that if we had presented them with battery they were resolved to parley, and so, by consequence, to yield, and this was the main and chief reason of the Portuguese not joining with us. There is one reason to be alleged on the Portuguese behalf, and their love and favour to our proceedings; for though they showed not themselves forward upon the occasion aforesaid in aiding us, yet they opposed not themselves as enemies against us. For had they pursued.us in our retreat from Lisbon to Cascaes, our men, being weak, sickly, without powder, shot, and other arms, they had put us to a greater loss and disgrace than we had on't. And if ever England have occasion to set up a competitor in Portugal, our good treatment of the people of that country has gained us great reputation amongst them; for the general most wisely forbade the rifling of houses in the country and suburbs of Lisbon, and commanded royal payment for everything they took, without compulsion or rigorous usage. This made those that were indifferently affected before now ready upon the like occasion to assist us."

In 1590, Elizabeth allowed the sum £8,970 yearly for the repair of the Royal Navy.

- C H A P T E R   X -

SEA-FIGHTS OFF FLORES AND CAPE CORRIENTES, 1591

WE HAVE now to record one of the most brave and desperate naval engagements that had as yet occurred in the sea-service of England.

In 1591, Elizabeth employed her naval power against Philip II by endeavouring to intercept his West Indian treasures, as the chief source of that greatness which made him so formidable to his neighbours. With this view she fitted out a squadron to intercept the home-returning Plate fleet.

The command of this squadron was given to the Vice-Admiral of England, Lord Thomas Howard, K.G., who was restored in blood (though his father had been attainted and beheaded in 1572), and summoned to Parliament as Lord Howard de Walden.

His second in command was Sir Richard Grenville, who in 1585 had sailed from Plymouth with seven ships to Roanoke, where he left 108 men to form an English settlement. On this expedition there sailed the *Defiance*, Lord Howard; the *Revenge*, Sir R. Grenville; the *Nonpareil*, Sir Edward Donnie; the *Bonaventure*, Captain Cross; the *Lion*, Captain Fenner; the *Crane*, Captain Duffield; and the *Foresight*, Captain Thomas Vavasour, of Haslewood, in Yorkshire. The latter was a gentleman who had particularly distinguished himself in raising forces and equipping vessels to defend England and its queen against the Armada. To requite his zeal, and to show her regard for one of her maids of honour, who was a Vavasour, and her acknowledged kinswoman, Queen Elizabeth, who through her grandfather, Sir Thomas Bulleyn, was descended from Maude Vavasour, would never permit the chapel at Haslewood to be molested, and to this day, adds Sir Bernard Burke, it has continued a place for Catholic worship.

Howard sailed to the Azores, as being the most likely quarter to find the Plate fleet, as many vessels which lose their longitude, or require refreshments, bear up for Flores, a small island of the group, so named by the Portuguese from the multitude of flowers which covered it. The isle is thirty miles long by nine broad, and had two small towns, named Santa Cruz and Lagena.

In that solitary place Howard's squadron lingered for six months, the King of Spain having given orders that the fleet was to be as late as possible in sailing from the West Indies, thinking by this delay to weary the English, of whose departure he had heard, and compel them to return home. In the meantime, Don Alphonso Bassano, who was sent from Spain with fifty-three ships to convoy the fleet home, came so suddenly upon the little English squadron that the admiral had much difficulty in getting to sea, with more than half his men sick and unserviceable.

The first intelligence Lord Howard had of the Spaniards was by the *Moonshine*, which the Earl of Cumberland had dispatched from the Spanish coast, near which he was cruising, to report "that a great armada was getting ready at the Groyne to be sent against Her Majesty's ships waiting to surprise the "West Indian fleet." Hakluyt says that Captain Middleton, commander of the *Moonshine*, which was a swift sailer, kept company with this fleet from the Groyne, long enough to discover the strength of it; and then, outsailing it, brought the startling intelligence. It was in the afternoon of the 31st of August, 1591, that he boarded the admiral's ship off Flores and delivered his message; but he had scarcely done so, when the whole Spanish fleet appeared on the horizon !

And now ensued a most unequal battle, in which the first ship of war ever taken by the Spaniards was lost. The squadron gained the offing, all save the vice-admiral's ship, the *Revenge*, which was hemmed in between the isle of Flores and the fleet. There are two reasons assigned for this circumstance: one is, that Sir Richard Grenville lingered too long for his men, who were straggling on shore; another, that he was courageously obstinate, and would not make his escape by flight, or, as Camden has it, would not let the pilot steer the *Revenge* so that she should seem to turn her stern upon the enemy.

Though he had ninety sick men on board, he cleared away for battle, and strove to break through the Spaniards, on board of whose, fifty-three ships there were no less than 10,000 soldiers. In the annals of war, perhaps there is not a more unequal conflict. At three in the afternoon a close battle began. Many times - fifteen it is stated - the Spaniards boarded him, but they were always repulsed, and killed, or flung into the sea. At one and the same time he was laid aboard by the *St. Philip*, a seventy-eight-gun ship, of 1,500 tons, and four more of the largest in the Spanish fleet, crowded with soldiers, who by a cross fire of muskets and arquebuses, below and aloft, swept his deck. In some were 200, in others 500, and in some 800 troops, besides armed mariners. He had never less than two large galleons alongside, and these were relieved from time to time by fresh ships. The sun set, and darkness came on, but under the clear starry sky of the Azores, the unequal fight was maintained, with all the fury that religious rancour and national hate could inspire, with much of contemptuous triumph in the hearts of the English, and to the two former emotions was added a longing for vengeance in those of the Spaniards. In the beginning of the fight, the *George Noble*, of London, having received some large shot through her, fell under the lee of the *Revenge*, and her captain asked Sir Richard if he could in any way serve him, but as she was only a small victualling ship, Grenville bid him shift for himself and leave the *Revenge* to her fate.

Between three in the afternoon and daylight next morning did the single English ship maintain a close fight with fifteen of the largest vessels in Bassano's fleet, and, by the well-directed fire of her guns, sank four of them. Among these were their greatest galleon and the admiral of the hulks. Early in the action Sir Richard Grenville had received a wound, but he never left the upper deck till eleven at night, when he was again wounded in the body by a musket-ball, and then went below to have it dressed. He received another shot in the head while under the hands of the surgeon, who was killed by his side. He returned on deck, faint and weak, but high in spirit as ever, and still the fight went on. By daybreak his crew began to want powder, and soon the last barrel was expended. By repulsing such a succession of boarding parties, their pikes and swords were broken and otherwise destroyed; forty of the crew were killed out of one hundred and three, their original number, and all the rest were more or less wounded; the masts had been shot away, the whole rigging cut to pieces, and the ship had become an unmanageable hulk.

On finding her in this crippled condition when day dawned, Sir Richard proposed to the ship's company "to trust to the mercy of God, not to that of the Spaniards, and to destroy the ship with themselves - to die, rather than to yield to the enemy!"

To this desperate resolution the master-gunner and a few seamen consented, but the rest opposed it; so Grenville was compelled to surrender himself as a prisoner of war, and, after a fifteen hours' engagement, was carried on board the ship of Don Alphonso Bassano. By this time the *Revenge* had six feet of water in her hold, three shot-holes under water, and all her bulwarks beaten away. "She had been engaged not only with the fifteen ships that boarded her, but in reality with the whole Spanish fleet of fifty-three ships; she had received, upon a computation, 800 cannon-shot, and the fire of nearly 10,000 soldiers and seamen."

In this sharp and unequal action, the Spaniards lost four ships, more than 1,000 men, and several officers of distinction. Lord Howard would seem to have but indifferently seconded the desperate valour of Grenville. We are told that though his force was so small, he would have continued the engagement with the enemy, notwithstanding their vast superiority, had he not been dissuaded by his officers from an undertaking so rash. However, they fought bravely as long as they had the weather-gage, and did all that could be expected of them, till darkness came on, when the squadron bore off and left Grenville to his fate. Notwithstanding what has been said in excuse of these officers, says an old naval historian, it is more than probable that if they had behaved with the same vigour and resolution as Grenville and his ship's company did, "they might have given a good account of the Spanish fleet. At least the history of this reign furnishes us with more than one such example. It will be said they had on their side Necessity and Desperation, two violent spurs to urge them on; but every commander in the fleet might have made that his own case."

The very next day after this unfortunate action the Plate fleet, of fourteen sail, for which the English had waited so long, hove in sight of Don Alphonso's. Thus, had Howard stayed but one day longer, or had the fleet from the Groyne been one day or two later, the Indian squadron might have fallen into the hands of the English, with many millions of treasure, which the sea afterwards swallowed.

On the second day after the action, Grenville, whose valour was highly praised by the Spaniards, died of his wounds on board the ship of Bassano. His last words were: -

"Here die I, Richard Grenville, with a joyful and quiet mind; for that I have ended my life as a true Englishman ought to, fighting for his country, queen, religion, and honour; my soul willingly departing from this body, leaving behind the lasting fame of having behaved as every valiant soldier (sic) is, in his duty, bound to do."

Five days afterwards, the *Revenge*, having been refitted, perished off the isle of St. Michael, "making good her name," as she had 200 Spaniards on board; and the fourteen ships of the Plate fleet went down with her. On his homeward voyage, Lord Howard made some amends for his loss at the Azores by the capture of several rich Spanish ships. Among others, he took one bound for the West Indies, in which, besides much booty, were found 22,000 Indulgences for the Spaniards in America - documents on which the English sailors set but small value. We read that about the same time Thomas White, a Londoner, in another Spanish capture, found no less than 2,000,000 of similar papers. These had cost the King of Spain 300,000 florins; but he could have sold them for 5,000,000 in the Indies. Before Bassano attacked Lord Howard's squadron at Flores, the latter had taken at least twenty ships coming from St. Domingo, India, and Brazil. Among these were two literally laden with gold and silver, and all were sent to England. Lord Howard, says Sir William Monson, kept the sea so long as his provisions lasted, and by his prizes nearly defrayed the whole expense of the expedition.

Sir Richard Grenville was probably one of the Grenvilles of Wootton-under-Barnwood, in Buckinghamshire, where an honourable family of that name had existed from the time of Henry I.

Lord Thomas Howard for his services was afterwards created Earl of Suffolk, and installed a Knight of the Garter. The original plate of his installation still remains in the ninth stall at St. George's Chapel, Windsor. He was subsequently engaged with Lord Monteagle in the discovery of the Gunpowder Treason; became Lord High Treasurer of England; and died at a green old age, in 1626.

The next most memorable or interesting sea-fight of this year is one that occurred on the 13th of June, 1591, off Cape Corrientes, a bold and cliffy promontory on the coast of Cuba, between the Spaniards and four English ships, one of which was a small barque belonging to Sir George Carey. The latter, who was Marshal of Her Majesty's Household, Captain of the Isle of Wight, and was afterwards Lord Hunsdon, Lord Chamberlain, and Captain of the Honourable Band of Gentlemen Pensioners, would seem to have been cruising among the West Indian Isles, but whether on the queen's service or for his own personal profit is not very clear from Hakluyt.

It would appear that when off Corrientes, about five in the morning of the 13th of June, he discovered six Spanish ships, four of which were armados, then a general name for armed craft, viz., the admiral and vice-admiral, of 700 tons each, other two of 600, and two of 100 tons each. Believing them to be the Carthagena squadron, Sir George "bore up to them with joy," and with his own ship, the *Swallow*, and the *Hopewell*, came to leeward of the Spanish admiral, while the barque, which was named the *Content*, bore down upon the vice-admiral, "and ranging along by her broadside, a-weather of her, gave her a

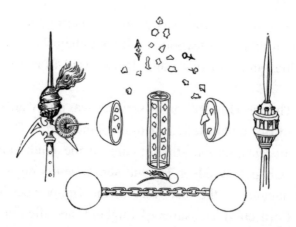

Chain-shot and firework weapons (end of the sixteenth century).

volley of their great guns and small-arms, and then coming up with another smaller ship, ahead of the former, hailed her in such a manner that she sheered off."

While engaging the latter ship, the crew of the *Content* saw with alarm clouds of smoke rising from the ship of Sir George Carey, and the *Swallow* (330 tons and 160 men) and *Hopewell* steering wide of him, with all the sail they could make. The *Content* bore towards him, to yield assistance if required; but in this movement fell to leeward of the two small vessels, who designed now to close in and board her; and then a three hours'engagement ensued between them. The *Content* had no great guns, but only one minion, or 4-pounder; one falcon, or 2-pounder; one saker, or 5-pounder; and two porte-bases. Her commander was Captain Nicholas Lisle; her crew consisted of only a lieutenant, master, master's mate, and twenty men.

This little barque, so slenderly manned and lightly armed, maintained a three hours'fight with the other two ships, who alternately drove her northward, no assistance being rendered her by either the *Hopewell* or *Swallow*. Meanwhile, Sir George Carey, after fighting for a time with the Spanish vice-admiral and another great ship, hoisted his top-gallant sails and all the other canvas he could spread, and stood off to sea. The *Hopewell* and *Swallow* had also failed to succour him, and were now standing off eastward, close-hauled.

The little craft, the *Content*, abandoned thus, had now the whole Spanish squadron to encounter. Three, however, only attacked, the two great ships and a smaller one, "they having a loom gale." The English now shipped their sweeps to row inshore, in hope of being able to anchor in shallow water, where the Spaniards dared not follow, and where they might be beyond range of their cannon.

On seeing this, the Spanish admiral double-manned one of his smaller vessels, and sent a boat ahead to tow her, in hope by their small-arms to shoot some of the English when at the oars or sweeps; but by the time the *Content* was within range of musket or arquebuse, a gale of wind had sprung up off shore, and the Spaniards being to leeward, the *Content* trimmed her canvas and stood due east. The small Spanish vessel had now crept within falcon-shot, while one of the great ships lay to the westward, so that Captain Nicholson, in his pigmy man-of-war, had no hope of escape in that direction.

Thinking he might avoid them by standing westward, he altered his course, but now the other great ship got under his lee, and the smaller one on his weather quarter, "purposing to make them pay room with the great ship, by force of her small and great shot."

By some skilful tacking and manoeuvring, they continued to make the 700-ton ship "spring her loof," or bring her head closer to the wind; and a fortunate shot from their saker pierced her between wind and water, so that her crew were compelled to careen her over, and summon assistance from the other ships.

The captain of the *Content* being now free in one quarter by the aid of the wind and the skill of his little crew, saw two sail more in the offing, which were hailed with cheers, as they were supposed to be the *Hopewell* and *Swallow*, long since out of sight, returning to their assistance. But they were painfully undeceived when they proved to be two more of the enemy's galleys; and, abandoned and surrounded thus, something like the sullen courage of despair rather than that which is gathered from hope, filled the hearts of those twenty-three unfortunate Englishmen, fighting for their lives, rather than liberty, as quarter was seldom asked or given by the Spaniards in these waters.

One of the strange galleys bore down on their lee when the evening sun was setting beyond Cape Corrientes, and fired six cannon-shot at them; closing in upon their starboard quarter, she next gave them the fire of five brass guns from her bow, but without doing damage, and then endeavoured to board; but the English fired so briskly with their small-arms that the Spaniards abandoned the attempt. They next tried it by the stern, but Nicholson threw a fire-ball among them, so the galley sheered off.

While still endeavouring to beat to seaward and escape, they saw the two galleys and a frigate bearing down upon them. Believing themselves lost now, they swore to fight it out to the last man, and, by shouts and derisive cheers, dared the Spaniards to board them.

One shot more was fired, but no closer attempt was made; and thus the swift little vessel continued a running fight with the ships and galleys from seven in the morning till eleven at night. In all that time only two men were wounded in the *Content*, and not a man killed. About two next morning they had a gale from the east-north-east, which proved the means of their escape. When day broke the Spanish squadron was far to leeward; and though they continued the chase till ten o'clock, the gallant little vessel escaped by her swift sailing beyond all pursuit.

In this flying skirmish she was engaged "for fifteen or sixteen hours with three Spanish armados, of 600 tons or 700 tons each, not being above musket-shot from any of them; and before the sun set there had come up two of the king's galleys to the fight. The armados fired continually at her with their great guns, not less than 500 times; and her sides, hull, and masts were literally sowed with musket-balls. Her sheets, tops, and shrouds were almost cut asunder with their great and small shot. Through her mainsail she had nineteen great shot; through her maintopsail four, through her foretopsail five, and through her mainmast one."

If all this be true, we cannot wonder at the sailors of Elizabeth, and those of later times, having a hearty contempt for the gunnery and seamanship of the Spaniards.

- C H A P T E R   X I -

LAST EXPEDITION AND DEATH OF ADMIRALS DRAKE AND HAWKINS, 1595

I N ENGLAND the rumour was universally gaining ground that Philip of Spain had designs of invading that country with a fleet more formidable even than the Great Armada of 1588. Hence the queen ordered two squadrons to be fitted out - one to cruise in the English seas, and another for service in America or the West Indies; while the King of Scotland, now in alliance with her, levied, in conjunction with England, troops against the Spaniards.

The foreign squadron consisted of twenty-six ships; but Sir William Monson only gives the names of the following: - *Defiance*, 500 tons, Sir Francis Drake, Commander; *Garland*, 700 tons, Sir John Hawkins; *Hope*, 600 tons, Captain Gilbert York; *Bonaventurc*, 600 tons, Captain Troughton; *Foresight*, 300 tons, Captain Winter; *Adventure*, 250 tons, Captain Thomas Drake.

The land forces were commanded by Sir Thomas Baskerville. Sir Nicholas Clifford was lieutenant-general; Captain Arnold Baskerville was sergeant-major; and there were Captain Nicholas Baskerville and eight other captains over the troops.

This West Indian expedition was specially urged upon the queen by the two admirals, Drake and Hawkins, who promised "to engage very deeply in the adventure, both with their substance and persons; and such was the opinion every one had conceived of these two valiant commanders, that great were the expectations of the success of this voyage."

Notwithstanding all the preparations for defence of the coast, and for the annoyance of the foe elsewhere, in the month of

July, 1595, a body of Spaniards suddenly landed in Cornwall, under the command of Don Diego Brojen, and burned Penzance, the church of St. Paul, which stood in the fields, and the fisher villages of Newlyn and Mousehole, and all without resistance. According to Carew, the inhabitants were infatuated by an old prediction in the Cornish language, to the effect that a period would arrive when

"Strangers would land
　　On the rocks of Merlin,
To burn Paul's Church,
　　Penzance, and Newlyn;"

but when the prophecy had been fulfilled, they found courage to assemble on the beach, and thus intimidate the Spaniards, who re-embarked, spread their sails to the breeze, and left the coast.

In the subsequent month the fleet of twenty-six sail, under Drake and Hawkins, left Plymouth Sound, but whether direct for San Juan de Porto Rico, where the queen was informed that vast treasures were collected for the King of Spain, or for Nombre

Spanish attack on Penzance.

de Dios, and thence to march to Panama, is uncertain now, for. after putting to sea the admirals would seem to have altered their plans. On the 31st of August they last saw the Lizard, and on the 27th of September were off Canaria Grande, the chief isle of the Canaries. They made a fruitless attempt to possess themselves of it. Hawkins was averse to landing at all, deeming it a loss of time to do so, and risking the chance of greater success elsewhere; but Drake and Baskerville, especially the latter, undertook to reduce the whole island in four days with the pikemen and musketeers. To their importunities, added to those of the seamen, who were already short of provisions, he was obliged to submit; but the attempt proved a failure. Afterwards they sailed for Dominica, one of the Antilles group; the right of occupancy there being claimed by England, France, and Spain, so that it remained a neutral island till 1759, when it was finally taken by Great Britain. The expedition arrived there on the 29th of October, and as the admirals stayed too long, building pinnaces and trafficking with the natives for tobacco, tidings of their coming spread from isle to isle, and the Spaniards everywhere prepared for defence.

On the very day of their arrival at Dominica, five Spanish ships which had been sent out to watch their motions, and convey the Plate fleet home from Porto Rico, captured a little English vessel, called the *Francis*, which had strayed from the fleet. By cruel and barbarous tortures, the Spanish officers wrung from her master and mariners a confession that the English had designs on Porto Rico; for which place they at once bore up, to give intelligence of an expected attack. The result was that the treasures of gold and silver were immediately buried, and small vessels were dispatched to all the isles and sea-coasts to give the Spanish colonists timely notice; so that when the admirals arrived off San Tuan de Porto Rico, on the 12th of November, it was so secured that they had little hope of success.

As soon as they came to anchor in the harbour - the same harbour where, in the subsequent year, the Earl of Cumberland was so nearly drowned by the weight of his armour - the enemy's batteries opened on them. On the Moro Fort alone were forty pieces of cannon. The fire was sharp and heavy; and that evening Sir Nicholas Clifford and Captains Browne and Strafford were all mortally wounded as they sat at supper with Admiral Drake, whose stool was knocked from under him by the same shot, just as he was in the act of drinking a can of beer.

The resistance of the Spaniards was desperate and protracted; and during the contest Sir John Hawkins died, it was alleged, of mortification and grief, consequent on some quarrels between him and the other commanders, according to one writer. Another states that he was extremely ill, and upon receiving intelligence that the *Francis* had been taken by the enemy, knew that the object of the expedition would be made known and frustrated, and that the bitterness of this conviction preyed upon his spirits.

The Spaniards had sunk a great ship at the mouth of the harbour, to bar the entrance; they had, moreover, formed two booms of large masts lashed firmly together thence to the forts, the guns of which protected the approach by a cross fire. Within the haven were five Spanish ships, anchored broadside-on, all ballasted with sand, mounted with great guns, and well manned by cannoniers and musketeers.

Undeterred by all these preparations, on the evening of the 13th, Sir Thomas Baskerville, with twenty-five boats and pinnaces full of pikemen and musketeers, clad in half-mail, or brigandines, pulled boldly into the roadstead, between the forts or castles, whence the Spaniards fired 185 cannon-shot upon them; and the circumstance of the shots being so minutely reckoned illustrates how slow the process of gunnery was still in war. His men were under a heavy fire of small-arms, too; nevertheless, he boarded sword in hand the five ships in succession (one was of

400 tons, the rest of 200), and set them all in flames. Moreover, "he did great damage to the admiral and vice-admiral. The ships had each twenty brass guns and 100 barrels of gunpowder on board. Their loading, which consisted chiefly of silk, oil, and wine, had been already secured, as likewise the treasure, which one of the prisoners confessed to be three millions of ducats, or five-and-thirty tons of silver."

The fight on both sides was obstinate and bloody; but after various assaults, which were repulsed, with great loss on the part of the English, but still greater on that of the Spaniards, of whom many were killed, burned, drowned, or taken prisoners, Baskerville and his squadron of boats drew off to the fleet. Sir Francis Drake now concluded that further attempts in that quarter would be futile, and sailed for the coast of Terra Firma.

On the 1st of December his fleet was off the town of La Hacha, in New Granada, a small place at the mouth of a river of the same name, which he burned and destroyed, though the inhabitants offered to purchase its ransom for 34,000 ducats.

He afterwards set fire to La Rancheria, where he took many negro slaves and other prisoners, with a vast quantity of pillage, including a great store of pearls." Advancing towards the Sierra de Santa Marta, he burned all the villages in the province, and also the town of that name. The next place he took was La Nombre de Dios, a place so named by Don Diego Niquero. Last says that at this time it had high wooden houses, "broad streets, and a fair church; that it lay from east to west, in the middle of a great wood." After a short resistance from the forts that defended the harbour, he laid the town in ashes, and destroyed all the shipping, which Hakluyt states consisted of frigates, barks, and galiots. He found no money in the town, but in a watch-tower near it, on the summit of a hill, he discovered "twenty sows of silver, two bars of gold, some pearls, money coined, and other pillage."

From this place a "body of 750 pikemen and musketeers, under Sir Thomas Baskerville, began their march towards Panama. He proceeded in that direction for several days, and on some of their marches they were sorely galled by sudden volleys of musketry from concealed parties in narrow defiles and dense forests; and finding, besides, their progress through a pass completely obstructed by the erection of a new fort, which they were too weak in number to storm, they began a retreat to their fleet, on board of which they arrived on the 2nd of January, 1596, many of them wounded, and all half-starved, and harassed with fatigue, and by the weight of their arms and iron accoutrements, after having marched half way to the Southern Sea.

Sir Francis Drake now proposed to make his way to Escudo de Veraguas, a small low island near the coast of New Granada, and thence to Porto-Bello. But before he could achieve this, he was seized with a bloody flux, a distemper which was greatly aggravated by a sense of bad success in the whole details of his voyage; so this great admiral, the Nelson of the Elizabethan age, died on the 28th of January, to the great sorrow of the seamen and soldiers.

"Sir Francis Drake," says Sir William Monson, "was wont to rule Fortune; but now finding his error, and the difference between the present strength of the Indies and what it was when he first knew them, grew melancholy upon this disappointment, and suddenly, and I hope naturally, died at Puerto-Bello," a mistake for Nombre de Dios. By the latter phrase, he would seem to insinuate a suspicion of suicide. He had no other funeral, than that which falls to the lot of those who die at sea., save that his remains were cased in a heavy coffin of lead, and then cast overboard, "with volleys of shot and firing of cannon in all the ships of the fleet; so he happened to find his grave near the place whence he had borrowed so large a reputation by his

Drake's funeral.

fortunate successes." He left a widow, Elizabeth, only daughter and heiress of George Sydenham, of Combe Sydenham, Devonshire. He bequeathed all his lands to his nephew, Captain Thomas Drake, except a single manor, which he left to his old shipmate, Captain Jonas Bodenham.

Both admirals now being dead, the command of the fleet devolved upon Sir Thomas Baskerville, who, in unison with the other officers, deemed a return to England their most prudent course. Proceeding on their homeward voyage, near Isla de Pinos (or Isle of Pines), off the southern coast of Cuba, from which it is separated by a channel sixteen leagues long and six leagues wide, they suddenly encountered the Spanish fleet of twenty sail, which had been sent out from Carthagena to intercept them, and had been hovering there for some time for that purpose.

Sir Thomas Baskerville, in the *Defiance*, and Captain Troughton, in the *Garland*, led the van in the engagement that ensued. It lasted two hours, and in the end the Spaniards, finding that one of their largest ships had been set on fire and burned to the water's edge, that several of the rest were severely wounded in their hulls and tattered in their sails arid rigging, sheered off, and the English fleet continued its voyage home. It arrived in England in the month of May, after having been out eight months, with but very little booty; and the destruction of a few towns and ships was deemed but a poor recompense for the loss of two of the greatest naval commanders in Europe. Moreover, this year proved fatal to the service in that respect, as it saw the deaths of other excellent seamen and commanders, such as Sir Roger Williams and Sir Thomas Morgan.

"Sir Francis Drake had an insatiable thirst after honour," wrote a gentleman of those days who served under him and Hawkins, and whose letter is quoted by Lediard. "He was full of promises, and more temperate in adversity than in prosperity.

He had likewise some other imperfections, such as quickness to anger, bitterness in disgracing, and was too much pleased with flattery. Sir John Hawkins had malice with dissimulation, rudeness in behaviour, and was covetous to the last degree. But they were both alike happy in being great commanders, yet not equally successful. They both grew great and famous by the same means; that is, by their own courage and the fortune of the sea. There was comparison, however, between their merits, taken in general, for therein Sir Francis far exceeded."

- C H A P T E R X I I -

THE CAPTURE OF CADIZ, 1596

THE BAD success of the last expedition of Drake and Hawkins led the English people to think of endeavouring to cripple the power of Spain nearer home than the Indies, especially as rumours of hostile preparation in all the Spanish harbours sounded once more the alarm of an invasion; and such an enterprise, on a grander scale even than the Armada, now filled the mind of Philip, who never forgave, even in her shrivelled old age, Elizabeth's refusal to marry him.

Firm, resolute, watchful, and self-controlled, the queen, whose policy had ever been to defend her own shores rather than to invade her neighbours', yielded to the suggestions of Lord Howard of Effingham, High Admiral of England, who urged upon her the prudence as well as the glory of attacking the enemy in his own ports, and at length succeeded, in spite of the opposition of Burleigh, in wringing from Elizabeth a reluctant consent. The King of Scotland was roused by the rumours of the new Armada, and, by a proclamation issued from Holyrood on the 2nd of January, commanded the forces of his kingdom "to hold themselves in readiness to march "(Rymer).

An expedition was accordingly prepared at Plymouth to avert the coming storm, and, strangely enough, English authors vary very much as to the number of ships employed. Burchett says the fleet consisted of 146 sail; Camden numbers it at 150, including twenty Dutch vessels, under Admiral John Van Duvenwoord, of Warmond; while in others the numbers vary still more.

The troops consisted of 7,360 pikemen and musketeers, of whom fully a thousand were volunteers, who paid their own expenses, and 6,762 seamen and cannoniers, besides the Dutch. Burchett states that the whole of these forces were under the command of Robert, Earl of Essex, the rash and daring favourite of Elizabeth's old age, whom she beheaded five years afterwards, in his thirty-fourth year. He and Howard from their own purses spent vast sums on the equipment of the troops and ships; and they were assisted by a Council of War, consisting of Lord Thomas Howard, Sir Walter Raleigh, Sir Francis Vere (the hero of the Low Country wars), Sir George Carew and Sir Conyers Clifford. The admiral was to command at sea, and Essex on the coast of Spain.

The fleet was divided into four squadrons. The admiral led the first, Essex the second, Lord Howard the third, and Raleigh the fourth. The officers of the army, under Essex, were Sir Francis Vere, with the proud tide of Lord Marshal; Sir John Wingfield, Campmaster-General; Sir Conyers Clifford, Sergeant-Major (i.e., Adjutant-General); Sir George Carew, Master of the Ordnance. The colonels of foot were Robert, Earl of Sussex, Sir Christopher Blount, Sir Thomas Gerrard, and Sir Richard Wingfield. The captain of the volunteers was Sir Edward Wingfield; and Andrew Ashley was Secretary at War, to keep a register of the councils: and in these details we see the gradual development of that internal order and discipline which reached such perfection in more modern times.

The queen's ships numbered only fourteen, and were as follow: - The *Ark Royal*, 800 tons, Captain Sir Amyas Preston, with the High Admiral on board; *Repulse*, 700 tons, Captain Sir William Monson, with the Earl of Essex on board; *Mary Honora*, 800 tons, Captain the Lord Thomas Howard; *Warspite*, 600 tons, Captain Sir Walter Raleigh; *Lion*, 500 tons, Captain Sir Robert Southwell; *Rainbow*, 500 tons, Captain Sir Francis Vere; *Nonpareil*, 500 tons, Captain Sir Robert Dudley; *Vanguard*, Captain Sir J. Wingfield; *Mary Rose*, 600 tons, Captain Sir George Carew; *Dreadnought*, 400 tons, Captain Sir Alexander Clifford; *Swiftsure*, 400 tons, Captain Sir Robert Cross;

Aquittance, 200 tons, Captain Sir Robert Mansfield; *Crane*, 200 tons, Captain King; *Tramontana*, captain's name not given.

The "Instructions to the Captains of Ships," &c, for this expedition are not without interest, as illustrative of the good order that was to be enforced.

First, God was to be served by the use of the common prayers twice daily; swearing, brawling, and diceing were forbidden; likewise "picking and stealing;" provisions were to be carefully issued, 'and weekly returns sent in. The ships were to be washed and cleaned daily; the fleet to close in at nightfall; the red cross half-hoisted was the signal of a council on board the two leading ships; care was to be taken that no jealousy occurred between the mariners and soldiers; the night-watch to be set by sound of drum or trumpet, at eight p.m.; guns to be fired and drums beaten in cases of fog; no man to strike 'his superior officer, under penalty of death; and no evil rumours to be raised adverse to the reputation "of any officer or gentleman."

On the 1st of June, 1596, this well-ordered array sailed from Plymouth, and ere long a breeze from the north-east brought them off the north cape of Spain. Every captain had sailed with sealed orders, which were not to be opened until they were past the scene of later days of glory - Cape St. Vincent - and this is the first record in history of English ships receiving such orders. On being opened, the general rendezvous was found to be - Cadiz !

The *Litness*, the *Truelove*, and the *Lion's Whelp*, three of the swiftest little vessels in the fleet, were now sent ahead as scouts, under Sir Richard Levison and Sir Christopher Blount, who kept pretty far from the coast; but succeeded on the 10th of June in capturing three Hamburg fly-boats, which fourteen days before had left Cadiz, where their skippers reported that all was quiet, and no attack suspected.

On the 18th they hailed an Irish ship returning from Cadiz,

whose master reported "that the Spaniards lived there in the most tranquil security. He informed them that the port was full of men-of-war, galleys, galleons, and merchantmen, richly loaded for the Indies; and that there were no forces on the island (DeLeon) except the garrison."

Flushed with the hopes of conquest and spoil," the fleet bore on, and about daybreak on the morning; of the 20th of Tune it was off Cadiz, where an alarm was speedily given. It had been previously arranged by the Council of War that a landing should be effected at San Sebastian, to the westward of the city; and there the whole fleet came to anchor in four squadrons, attended by their victuallers and other ships. Armour was buckled and matches were blown, and every soldier was prepared to land; but the wind almost blew a gale, the sea was running high, and four great galleys were lying off the shore to fire upon their boats; so no landing was made, and the day was passed in sending messages from ship to ship, chiefly borne by Sir Walter Raleigh, concerning the course to be next decided upon; and, in the end, the leaders came to the resolution of attacking the shipping, and making themselves masters of the harbour before a landing was attempted.

The city, it must be borne in mind, is situated on the extremity of a long tongue of land, projecting in a north-westerly direction from the Isle of Leon. At its end the tongue expands a little, and the whole of this expansion is occupied by the city. This isthmus is so narrow that the waves of the Atlantic on one side, and those of the bay on the other, reach the walls of the causeway which connects Cadiz with the mainland of Andalusia. Its castle, built by the Moors, was strongly fortified, and four other great bastions defended the bay, which is several miles in extent. It was considered the key of Spain, and was one of the three towns which the Emperor Charles V advised his son Philip to have ever a watchful eye upon.

A dash into the harbour being determined on, a contention arose, curiously, as to who was to lead the way. Asserting his commission, the Earl of Essex claimed the honour; to this the admiral objected, being aware that if the rash young earl failed, the expedition would be futile. Moreover the old queen, in her maudlin love for him, had strictly forbidden him "to expose himself to danger, but upon great necessity" - rather odd advice to give to a leader of those sword-in-hand days. It was ultimately arranged that next morning the ships that were the fleetest sailers and drew the lightest draught, under Lord Thomas Howard, Raleigh, Southwell, Vere, Carew, and Cross, with a few others, should dash in and perform this service, by driving from its moorings the Spanish fleet of fifty sail which lay across the bay.

With the first blink of dawn and with a favourable wind they bore inward, passing the fire of the Muelle de San Felipe, and attacked the Spanish fleet. "Here did every ship strive

The English fleet before Cadiz.

to be headmost," says Sir Walter Raleigh; "but such was the narrowness of the channel that neither the admiral nor any other ship could pass one by another. There was command given that no ship should shoot but the queen's, making account that the honour would be the greater that was obtained by so few." Steering his ship in mid-channel, Sir Walter Raleigh ran the bows of the *Warspite* with a terrible crash against one Spanish galleon, and, pouring the fire of his forecastle guns upon her, drove her from her anchors. Sir Francis Vere, eager to lead the way on one element as bravely as he had ever done on the other, turned the guns and small-arms of the *Rainbow* on the galleys; but the latter being anchored under the protection of the city batteries, he was very roughly handled till Essex stood in to his relief.

Then it was that several of the Spanish ships sought to escape by creeping along shore to the bottom of the bay, to where the Isle de Leon is joined to the mainland by a bridge, which an old work states to have been 700 paces long. This is called the San Pedro Channel, an arm of the sea with a strong tide running through it. It is from 200 to 500 yards wide, is deep and muddy, and nowhere fordable even at the lowest tide. The bridge, which consists of five arches, is called the Puente de San Pedro; and the city can never be captured from the land while its inhabitants are masters of the bay. By this narrow channel many of the Spanish ships escaped, Lediard says, "by the help of a machine," which probably was a drawbridge, till the entrance was made secure by Sir John Wingfield, in the *Vanguard*.

Meanwhile, many of the great galleons and galleys kept their anchorage at the Puntals, receiving the broadsides of the English, and returning them with interest, till noon; the Earl of Essex, the high admiral, and his son, being now in the heat of the action, which gradually proved favourable to the English. The Spanish ships became so miserably shattered - in some instances masts and bulwarks being shot away, two or three port-holes beaten into one - and so many of their crews were killed or wounded, that they became no longer either tenable or defensible. So their officers set many of them on fire, and scuttled others, sinking them with such precipitation that, though some of their men endeavoured to escape to the shore by boats, by far the greater number flung themselves into the sea, where some were rescued by the English, on their calling for "quarter," but others especially the soldiers and cannoniers, who were accoutred with back, breast, and head-pieces of iron, were miserably drowned, some being sucked into the vortex of many a sinking ship.

Amid this hurly-burly, the *San Philipo*, of 1,500 tons, the Spanish admiral's ship, was blown up - one account says by a revengeful Moorish slave, who fired the powder-room; another by her own officers, rather than let her become the prize of the English - but by the explosion she destroyed three great ships that lay near her. One English ship was burned, and one Dutch, by her own powder, was blown up. ("History of Holland," London, 1705).

The Dutch by this time, under their admiral, Van Duvenwoord, had bravely attacked and carried the Puntals; while the Earl of Essex landed a body of troops at a point between that place and the city, which the ships were now assailing from the seaward. Sir Francis Vere, in his Commentaries, quaintly describes the landing thus:-

"On the right hand, in an even front, with a competent distance betwixt the boats, were ranged the two regiments first named "(Essex's corps and his own), "the other three (being those of Sir Christopher Blunt, Sir Thomas Gerrard, and Sir Conyers Clifford) on the left, so that every regiment and company of men were sorted, together with the colonels and chief officers, in nimble pinnaces, some at the head and some at the stern, to keep good order. The general himself, with his boat, in which it pleased him to have me to attend him, and some other boatsful of gentlemen adventurers and choice persons to attend his person, moved a pretty distance before the rest, when, at a signal given at a drum from his boat, the rest were to follow, according to the measure and time of the sound of the said drum, which they were to observe in the dashing of their oars; and to that end there was a great silence, as well of warlike instruments as otherwise, which order being duly followed, the troops came altogether to the shore, and were landed (i.e., by rowing to the beat of the drum), and several regiments embattled in an instant, without any encounter at all, the Spaniards, who, the day before, had showed themselves with troops of horse and foot on that part, as resolved to impeach our landing, being returned to the town."

In other words, the troops landed with flying colours, and unopposed, half a mile to the eastward of Cadiz, and half that distance from the narrow neck of land which connects one portion of the Isle de Leon with the other; while the fleet, under the Howards, was taking, burning, sinking, or driving on shore and utterly destroying, the nucleus of the new Armada of Spain; work which lasted till four in the afternoon, says Sir Walter Raleigh.

As the four regiments now landed mustered only 2,000 men, and the city was strongly fortified by walls which extended from sea to sea, it was deemed imprudent to attempt anything further than the occupation of sufficient ground whereon to bivouac; but as the column advanced inland, a bolder policy, of which Vere is confessed on all hands to have been the suggester, was adopted. Perceiving that crowds of people on foot and on horseback were passing from the island into the town by a road that skirted the opposite side of the steep promontory, he urged its immediate occupation by a body of troops. Essex instantly adopted the advice, and sent the regiments of Clifford, Blunt, and Gerrard on this service, giving them strict orders also "to break down the bridge and the engine which had secured the escape of the galleys;" and this was all promptly done, while at the same time Essex and Vere continued to advance with something less than a thousand combatants under their orders.

Among these were Lodovick, Count of Nassau (who was afterwards defeated and slain by Don Sancho de Avila); the Earl of Sussex; William Herbert, son of the Earl of Worcester; Bourke, an Irish chief; Sir Christopher St. Lawrence; Sir Robert Drury, and others, all men of rank, and possessed of considerable influence.

As they drew nearer Cadiz, the Spaniards were seen ready to meet them, arrayed in front of the ditch, "with cornets, and ensigns displayed, and thrusting out some loose horse and foot, as it were to provoke a skirmish." Essex had never conceived that a place so strong by art and nature as the city of Cadiz could be reduced in any other manner than by a protracted and vigorous siege; but somehow the aspect and conduct of the Spaniards led the ardent and energetic Sir Francis Vere to believe that the city might be won sooner than they could have hoped. If he could possibly help it, the attempt should be made without delay.

"These men now standing in battle before the ditch," said he to Essex, "will show and make the way into the town for us this night if they be well handled."

In consequence of this, the manner of "handling" them was entirely committed to him, and he lost no time in issuing his orders, and planning his mode of attack.

The approach to Cadiz in the direction pursued by the English was then, and to some extent is still, through the midst of a succession of sandy hillocks, well adapted to the purpose of concealing small bodies of troops, though inadequate to mask the movements of a large column. Vere formed his force into three divisions, the first consisting of 200 men, the second of 300, and the third of 500. Led by Sir John Wingfield, the first was ordered to assail the Spaniards briskly with pike and musket, and engage them in a desultory skirmish. The second, under Sir Matthew Morgan, was to follow in support at a moderate distance, but on no account to close to the front till the proper crisis should arrive; while the third and -last, being under the immediate guidance of Essex and Vere, acted as a reserve. Thus it will be seen that Sir Francis Vere had rightly understood the relative positions of besieged and besiegers.

When each officer had been fully instructed, Sir John Wingfield led on the first division, which, as Vere expected, was furiously assailed by the Spaniards, and fell back in apparent confusion, drawing on the pursuers till they reached the hillock where Morgan was posted. The second corps instantly charged, upon which the garrison, taken completely by surprise, fled with such precipitation that their officers were incapable of rallying them, even under the guns of the city. They plunged, tumbled, or rolled into the ditch, which, though deep and wide, was dry; they scrambled in scores up the steep face of the unscarped rampart, promptly followed by the first and second divisions; while the men of the reserve, coming on at a rush, had also flung themselves into the ditch. One party aided their comrades by scaling a portion of the main wall, while another select band of stormers, under an officer of tried courage, poured silently but swiftly along the ditch till they came to a place destitute of guards, and more than ordinarily accessible. Through this they made good their entrance, led by Lieutenant Evans, Arthur Savage, and Samuel Bagnal, "who bravely leaped from an eminence of a pike's length, to be first in the town," and boldly advancing to the scene of action, speedily cleared the rampart of its defenders. Pell-mell the assailants now rushed in, with levelled pikes and clubbed muskets; and a fierce hand-to-hand battle raged in all the streets and by-lanes of the city, until the marketplace was reached.

By this time a body of seamen had poured in, led by the Howards, Sir Walter Raleigh, Sir William Paget, Sir Robert Southwell, Sir Robert Mansel (afterwards vice-admiral under James and Charles I.), Richard Levison, and Sir Philip Wodehouse, of Kimberley; and with them came Sir Edward Hobby, carrying the colours of England. Both parties now met in the streets, when a heavy fire was maintained on them from the windows and housetops. The Casa de Ayuntimiento, or town-hall, was now stormed by Vere, at the head of 300 men; he cleared it of a body of the garrison who had taken possession of it, and the market-place was finally scoured; but there Sir John Wingfield, who had bravely performed his part in the assault, was shot through the head and slain. Savage and Bagnal, who were covered with wounds and blood, were knighted on the spot.

The storming of Cadiz.

Vere now compelled a more numerous force in the abbey of St. Francis to surrender and so environed a battalion in Fort San Felipe, that when summoned the gates were opened. "Thus, by his good conduct," says Vere's biographer, "was a conquest secured, the first attainment of which may be traced to his gallantry; for except the battalion which followed himself, there were not, within ten minutes after the assault, forty men in one mass throughout the entire compass of the city."

A contribution was levied upon the inhabitants, and great booty acquired; but not a single life was taken in cold blood, and no woman had to complain of suffering insult from any English seaman or soldier - a praiseworthy forbearance, rare in those days. Under a guard, all the Spanish women were sent to Santa Maria, a place of safety, in English ships; and the men, to the number of 5,000. were disarmed and expelled - a treatment of prisoners of war which is worthy of special remark.

Many of the ladies quitted Cadiz in their richest apparel, with all their jewels on; while the Earl of Essex stood in person by the water-side, to see them safely embarked. Sir Francis Vere tells us that "he got three prisoners worth 10,000 ducats; one a churchman and President of Contradutation of the Indies, the others two ancient knights." This admission shows that the old practice, by which individuals were allowed to ransom their own prisoners, was not, as yet, obsolete.

By the capture of Cadiz, the King of Spain lost in shipping, provisions, and stores, destined for a new expedition against England, more than twenty millions of ducats. Besides the merchantmen, he lost two great galleons, which were captured with above 100 brass guns in them, thirteen other men-of-war, eleven ships freighted for the Indies, and eleven for other ports; and Stow has it that 1,200 pieces of ordnance were taken or sunk in the sea. Camden gives the names of sixty English gentlemen who were knighted for bravery on this occasion. All the commanders were enriched by plunder, with the exception of the Earl of Essex, who appropriated nothing but a noble library which he found in a public building.

A difference of opinion now arose among the leaders as to what was to be done with their new conquest. Sir Francis Vere insisted on the good policy of retaining the town; and offered, if left with only 4,000 men, to defend it against all the power of Spain (see his Commentaries). But his wish was not accepted; and it was resolved in the end to retire, after demolishing the defences and burning the houses. The artillery, stores, and general plunder were put on board of the fleet, which sailed after the troops were re-embarked, and Cadiz was left reduced to a heap of cinders overlooking a wreck-strewn shore; for the Duke of Medina, the Spanish admiral, while the assault was at its height, and the town was in the act of being captured, had beached a vast number of vessels and destroyed them by fire, to prevent them becoming prizes of the English.

All on fire for further glory, Essex now proposed to steer for the Azores, and there lie in wait for the East India caracks, on their homeward voyage; but, save Lord Thomas Howard and the Dutch admiral, no officer in the fleet would consent to such a movement.

The result of the attack on Cadiz filled Philip of Spain with greater fury than ever. Disappointed in all his projects for vengeance on the English by invasion, he found himself unable to defend even the shores of Spain. To revenge the losses he had last sustained at Cadiz, and to recover in some measure his tarnished glory, he was determined to make another effort ere the year 1596 came to a close, and ordered all his ships to rendezvous in the roads of Lisbon. He hired all the foreign ships that were in Spanish ports, and embarked on board of them a large body of newly-levied troops, together with a number of Irish refugees, at the port of Ferrol, in order to effect a landing in Ireland or England. But as soon as the fleet sailed, a tempest scattered it, destroying one-half and rendering the other completely unserviceable, so that Philip had to relinquish all ideas of aggression for the time; while Elizabeth, the further to secure England against any such attempts for the future, gave orders to strengthen and fortify Sandsfort, Portland, Hurst, Southsea, Calshot, St. Andrews, and St. Maudits.

About the middle of August, the troops from Cadiz were disembarked at the Downs, near Sandwich, and were, after the fashion of the times, when standing armies were scarcely known, immediately disbanded, save the regiments which Vere had brought from the Low Countries, and these were sent back to their original stations; the remainder returned to their homes, to tell in many a secluded English village the story of the capture of Cadiz.

- C H A P T E R X I I I -
PORTO RICO, 1598

ONE OF the most remarkable occurrences of the year 1598 was the tenth and last privateering expedition of George Clifford, the famous and adventurous Earl of Cumberland, against the Spaniards. His father had been raised to an earldom in 1525, by Henry VIII, and he was the first English subject who ever built a ship so large as 800 tons burden; and this vessel he employed in many actions against Spain, particularly in the West Indian seas.

It was in his favour that the venerable Sir Henry Lee, of Ditchley - than whom, perhaps, no knight of chivalry was more thoroughly imbued by the spirit of old romance - resigned, on the 17th of November, 1590, the anniversary of the queen's accession, the office of champion and president of a society which he had formed for promoting the exercise of arms.

No European prince ever possessed such vast resources as Philip II, of Spain. In addition to his Spanish and Italian dominions, the Kingdom, of Portugal, and the States of the Netherlands, he was master of the whole East Indian commerce, and reaped the richest harvest of ores from his South American mines. But his mighty armaments against England, his intrigues with France, and his long and aggressive wars in the Low Countries, enriched those whom he sought to subdue; while the Spaniards, dazzled by the sight of the precious metals, and elated with the idea of vast wealth, neglected the agriculture of Spain; its ingots and wedges of gold were no sooner coined than called for; while the interception of his Plate fleets and the plunder of his colonies became the incessant occupation of the English sea-adventurers, until "Spanish "became a term synonymous with money or treasure.

Lord Cumberland's expedition in 1598 was the largest he had ever fitted out, and was the greatest that any English subject had as yet set upon the sea. Several of the fleet were his own vessels, equipped entirely by his private purse, and without any assistance from the queen.

Including a vessel called *The Old Frigate*, and two barges for landing troops, the armament consisted of twenty sail. The leading ship, the *Scourge of Malice*, was commanded by the earl himself as admiral; the *Merchant-Royal* was commanded by Sir Tom Berkeley, as vice-admiral and lieutenant general. "There were besides, a noble train of commanders and other gentlemen for the land service."

On the 6th of March these adventurers sailed from Plymouth, to improve their fortunes on the high seas and among the Spanish colonies; and they had not long lost sight of the white cliffs of England before they received intelligence from a passing ship of five great caracks that were speedily to set sail from Spain with more wealthy cargoes than ever before had gone to the Indies, and that they were accompanied by five-and-twenty vessels bound for Brazil. In every ship of the squadron the most active preparations were made for meeting and attacking them, but made in vain; for the Spaniards had no sooner heard that Lord Cumberland was on the sea, than caravels of advice ran along the coast to prevent all ships of importance leaving their harbours. So the earl, who does not seem to have been particular as to what flag a ship carried, had to console himself by taking a Hamburger laden with corn, copper, and powder, and a French vessel laden with salt.

Finding that it was in vain to wait for the caracks or the Brazilian ships, the earl bore on with his whole fleet for the South Cape, capturing on the way "two Flemmings "laden with corn. In a few days he was off the Canary Isles, and effected a landing on Lanzerota, which is thirty-six miles long by fifteen broad, and contains several volcanoes. He anchored his whole fleet in the roadstead, which lies on the south-east of the island. In this solitary part of the world, a wealthy Spanish marquis had built for himself a strong castle of stone, defended by ramparts and brass cannon, flanked, and situated in a good position. In this place he had 200 guards and servants. This retinue enabled him to tyrannise like a petty king over all the inhabitants of the isle and of the adjacent one, of Fuerteventura, from which it is separated by the channel De Bocagna.

Sir John Berkeley advanced against this stronghold at the head of 600 pikemen and musketeers; and though twenty men might have held the keep against them, as the entrance was in the upper story, by ladders which were drawn in, the little garrison abandoned it, "and ran like bucks, leaving it a prey to the English, so terrible was the very name of the English to them at that time."

The arms of the natives were lances and stones. When a musketeer levelled his weapon at them, they threw themselves flat on the ground, and the moment he fired, they sprang up, hurled their missiles, and fled. The town, consisting of a hundred houses, roofed with canes and mud hardened in the sun, was pillaged of all that was worth taking; and also "an old tattered church," which had an altar at one end, but was without chancel or vestry. Sailing thence on the 21st of April, on the 23rd of May the fleet was off Dominica and the Virgin Isles, where the earl remained a month. Helanded mustered all his men, and announced to them that his next desire was to capture San Juan de Porto Rico, the attempt in which Drake had failed so recently, and the intelligence was greeted by reiterated cheers.

On the 6th of June he was off this island, which is the most eastern of the Great Antilles, and his plan of attack differed from that of Drake. He landed 1,000 men at a considerable distance from the town; and, seizing a negro, "who was half frightened to death, for their guide," marched towards it. Both the earl and Sir John Berkeley were in complete armour. Their way, we are told, was by steep cliffs and rugged rocks, till they reached an arm of the sea about a musket-shot in breadth, which separated them from the town, and where they found themselves exposed to the fire of a fort.

Opposite, on a slope, rose San Juan, on an isle, or isthmus rather, about half a league long, "fairly built, neat, and strong, after the Spanish manner. It had several large streets, was bigger than Portsmouth, was more agreeable to the eye, and had a good monastery and a cathedral what diminished from the whole was the want of glass, as they had only canvas or wooden shutters in their windows" ("Atlas Geographus," London, 1717). Its port was deemed by the Spaniards as the key of South America.

Powder-flasks and spanners for officers of horse. The lower for infantry (end of sixteenth century).

Cumberland's force was without boats by which to cross the little strait, and for a time he and his other captains were much perplexed, till a communication was discovered between the city and the mainland, by means of a narrow causeway that led to a bridge which was drawn up. Beyond this bridge was a strong barricade, and higher up was the fort, whence the Spaniards swept the causeway with ordnance and small-arms. This causeway was so rough and difficult to traverse, that the English preferred to wade through the sea by the side of it. A very dark night had succeeded a hot and brilliant day, when the attack was resolved on, "and though the earl was carried away very ill, by a fall from the causeway into the sea, when the weight and encumbrance of his armour nearly drowned him," his soldiers pressed on with ardour, passed then draw-bridge in the sea, which came up to their waist-belts, and assailed the gate of the barricade with their bills and hatchets; but so stout was the resistance of the Spaniards, and so heavy their fire upon the English, who were compelled to fight in the water, that the assailants were forced to retire.

The next attack was attended with better success; and, flushed with rumours of the gold mines that were alleged to be in the rocky parts of the isle, and the precious ore found in the sand of its rivers, Cumberland's men advanced with fresh ardour. While a party of musketeers, levelling their weapons over rocks or their rests, picked off the Spanish cannoniers at their guns, another, which was composed of pikemen and musketeers, was set ashore on the other side, midway between the fort and town. Finding their retreat about to be cut off, the garrison of the former were compelled, after a sharp resistance; to abandon it, and fell back on the town; but this they soon after deserted.

El Moro, a place of great strength, together with the strong castle in the western part of the town, and a third fort between it and the Moro, all surrendered in quick succession to the adventurous earl, who then found himself in undisturbed possession of the place.

He now resolved to retain it, to increase its fortifications, and to make it a point whence fleets might cruise against the Spaniards, now deemed, as the Scots had been for centuries, the natural enemies of England. This plan met with the warm approval of his followers; and a roll was prepared of those who volunteered to remain there as the nucleus of an English colony and garrison. In furtherance of this great scheme, the earl ordered all the Spanish inhabitants to depart to other isles, notwithstanding the offers they made him of rich goods and gold and silver plate, to be permitted to remain.

But an unforeseen misfortune came, in the form of a deadly sickness that decimated his slender force. Of the 1,000 men who landed, Camden records that 700 died, exclusive of those slain by the Spaniards. This mortality so scared the survivors, who were led to expect the same fate, that all resolved to quit the island as speedily as possible. The earl wished, ere doing so, to make some profitable terms with the Spaniards for its ransom. To these proposals they pretended to listen, and several messages passed between them and the earl; but the negotiations proceeded so slowly that he began after a time to perceive that they were only seeking to delay till death had further weakened his force, and to suspect that they had some treacherous design on foot.

While these negotiations were pending, there came into the harbour of San Juan a caravel from Margarita, an island of Venezuela, in the Caribbean Sea, with passengers bound for Spain; and these were very much surprised to find the island of Porto Rico in possession of the English. In the caravel the earl found pearls to the value of a thousand ducats; and learning from her crew that the pearl-chest at Margarita was very slenderly guarded, he sent three ships of his fleet to seize it. In the rich pearl-fishery there the Spaniards employed vast numbers of negroes from Guinea; and Lait records that they forced these wretched slaves to such excessive labour, that many killed themselves in despair, while others were drowned and maimed by sharks. But great though the prize looked for at Margarita, the earl's ships were driven back by adverse winds, and he, now becoming more than ever convinced that the Spaniards of the captured island had some ulterior and, perhaps, savage ends in view, sailed from Porto Rico with less than half his fleet, in search of fortune elsewhere, leaving Sir John Berkeley with the other half of his armament, and full power to act in his absence.

The separation took place on the 14th August The earl hoped to be in time to intercept the Mexican home-fleet, or some of the East Indian caracks off the Azores, but he came there too late, luckily for himself perhaps, as but a few days before his arrival at Flores, no less than twenty-nine large Spanish men-of-war had been there. How long Sir John stayed at Porto Rico after the earl is uncertain, and what terms he made with the colonists are unknown; but after a dreadful storm, in which all their vessels nearly perished, and were severely damaged, the fleet was reunited at Flores, and eventually returned to England in the month of October.

The earl held possession of Porto Rico for only forty days, but in that time he collected and brought away a vast quantity of hides, ginger, and sugar; eighty pieces of cannon; some ammunition; the bells of the churches; and a thousand ducatoons' worth of pearls. This is the general account given of the results of the expedition; but it is supposed that, as a matter of fact, he collected a much greater quantity of plunder, in the form of ingots and gold dust.

He lost only sixty men at the storming of Porto Rico; but forty were drowned in *The Old Frigate*, in a storm off Ushant.

The character of the Earl of Cumberland, is tersely

Attack on Porto Rico.

summarised by an old naval historian, who speaks of him as "a man of admirable qualities, both in civil and military affairs. He knew as well how to fight as to govern, and had virtues capable of rendering him equally illustrious both in war and peace. He was so excellent a person that it can hardly be said what was lacking in him, and yet he had one very considerable want, viz., a steady gale of good fortune; and, considering the vast expenses he was at, in building, hiring, and furnishing ships, it is a question whether his expeditions increased his estate."- His earldom became extinct in the year 1643.

IN THE BAY OF CEZIMBRA, 1602

THE LAST but one important event in the long and stirring reign of Elizabeth was the great sea-fight in the roadstead of Cezimbra, between her ships and those of the Spaniards. A rich carack of which the former were in pursuit had taken shelter there. "The harbour," says Hume, "was guarded by a castle; there were eleven galleys stationed in it. and the militia of the country, to the number of 20,000 men, appeared in arms upon the shore; yet, notwithstanding these obstacles, and others derived from the winds and tides, the English squadron broke into the harbour, dismounted the guns of the castle, sunk, burned, or put to flight the galleys, and obliged the carack to surrender. They brought her home to England, and she was valued at a million of ducats; a sensible loss to the Spaniards, and a supply still more important to Elizabeth."

The details of this gallant sea-fight, as given by one of the commanders, and other authorities, are as follow: -

To prevent the Spaniards from invading the coast of Ireland, the queen fitted out a squadron of eight ships of war, which she placed under the- command of Monson and Levison, who, since the death of Drake and Hawkins, were deemed the most skilful officers in the English navy. These vessels were the *Repulse*, Sir Richard Levison, Admiral; the *Garland*, Sir William Monson, Vice-Admiral; the *Defiance*, Captain Gore; the *Mary Rose*, Captain *Slingsby*; the *Warspite*, Captain Sommers; the *Dreadnought*, Captain Manwaring; the *Adventure*, Captain Trevor; and an English caravel, Captain Tawkell.

The Dutch had promised to aid the queen with twelve ships of war, that together they might scour the seas and molest the

Spaniards. The new expedition was prepared in great haste, so much so, that the squadron was not fully equipped either with men, ammunition, or provisions; when, on the 19th of March, 1602, Sir Richard Levison set sail with five vessels, leaving his vice-admiral, Monson, with three, to await the arrival of the Hollanders. Ere the latter arrived, and three days after Levison's departure, Sir William received a dispatch from the queen to go to sea with all speed, as she had received tidings that the Plate fleet was off the Isle of Terceira.

Sir William put to sea, with the *Garland* and two other ships, on the 26th of March, and stood down the Channel.

The queen's intelligence had been true, as the fleet had been at Terceira, which is the central island of the group named the Azores, but had shaped its course to Spain. On the voyage they were met by Sir Richard Levison, who, though the Spaniards mustered thirty-eight sail, bravely attacked them with his five. But being without Monson's vessels, and still more the twelve Hollanders, his bravery was exerted in vain, and he was beaten off, while the Plate fleet stood on its homeward course. Levison was naturally exasperated with the Hollanders for their delay, by which so much treasure escaped him. He now steered towards the Rock of Lisbon, which had been previously appointed by him as the place where he and Monson were to rendezvous; but Sir William having spent fourteen days cruising off the coast of Portugal, and seeing nothing of him, stood around the South Cape, "where he was likewise frustrated of a most pleasing expectation."

He came in sight of some ships, which showed the Scottish and French colours. These were merchantmen from San Lucar, where, as the Scottish skippers reported, there were five great galleons ready to sail with the next tide for India. They also told him that three days before two others had sailed, having on board Don Pedro de Valdez, the Governor of Havannah, and his retinue - the same Don Pedro who held a command in the Great Armada, and had been prisoner of war in England in 1588.

These two ships were met one night by Captain Sommers, in the *Warspite*; but, in consequence of the extreme darkness, and perhaps of their own strength, no engagement ensued.

This news of the five galleons at San Lucar, made Sir William Monson steer in the direction where he would be most likely to meet with them; and, in a shorter time than he anticipated, he discovered five ships, which he conceived to be, from the size and number, the identical galleons he was in quest of. But he was again doomed to disappointment, for on coming within gunshot they showed their colours, and proved to be English.

Next day he captured a Spanish Indiaman; "but he had better been without her, for she brought him so far to the leeward that the same night the five galleons passed to windward "unseen, and not above eight leagues off, as he was informed by the skipper of an English pinnace.

"These misfortunes," says Lediard, "lighting upon Sir Richard first and Sir William after, might have been sufficient reasons to discourage them; but they, knowing the accidents of the sea, and that Fortune could laugh as well as weep, and having good ships under foot, their men sound and in health, did not doubt that some of the wealth which the two Indies sent yearly to Spain would yet fall to their share."

On the 1st of June, the squadron, now united, was hovering off the Rock of Lisbon, as that round promontory in which the ridge of Cintra ends is named by seamen. There they, captured two Easterlings; and while overhauling their cargoes, they descried a caravel coming round Cape Espichel, a headland twenty-one miles south-west of Lisbon. She proved to be English, and reported to Sir Richard Levison that "a large carack, of 1,600 tons, was just arrived at Cezimbra, near St. Ubes, from the East

Indies, richly laden; and that there were eleven galleys in the same harbour, three of them Portuguese, under the command of Don Frederick Spinola, to cruise against the Dutch." Her master added that he had been sent with this message by the captains of the *Nonpareil* and *Dreadnought*, who were thereabout, looking out for the admiral.

With cheers and joy this news was received. Sir Richard immediately signalled Sir William to stand on with him, and, lest the signs should not be discerned, sent the caravel with a message to bear up for the roads of Cezimbra; but before they had rounded Cape Espichel night had closed in, and nothing took place but the exchange of a few cannon-shot between the admiral and the galleys of Spinola, who is called by Rymer a Genoese.

On the 2nd of June, when day dawned, "every man looked out early for what ships of Her Majesty were in sight," and there were but five - the *Warspite* (having the admiral on board, as the *Repulse* had become leaky, and been sent to England), the *Garland*, the *Nonpareil*, the *Dreadnought*, and the *Adventure*, besides the two Easterlings, with prize-crews on board.

A council, at which all the captains were present, was held on board the *Warspite*, and it lasted the most part of the day. Some alleged that it was impracticable to cut out the carack, defended as she was by eleven galleys, and lying close under the guns of the castle of Cezimbra; but Sir William Monson urged so vigorously that the attempt should be made - an attempt which he affirmed would be crowned with brilliant success - that it was resolved to make an attack next day, in the following manner.

He and Sir Richard were to come to anchor as near the carack as they could venture; the rest to keep under sail, and ply up and down without anchoring. Sir William Monson, we are told, was glad of this opportunity of having vengeance on these same galleys, "hoping to requite the slavery they had put him to when he was a prisoner in one of them."

He now sailed a league in front of the squadron, with his colours flying in defiance of the galleys. The Marquis of Santa Cruz and Frederick Spinola, the former general of the Portuguese,. and the latter of the Spanish galleys, accepted the challenge, and came out to fight him; but we are told that, "being within shot, they were diverted (from their purpose) by one John Bedford, an Englishman, who pretended to know the force of the ship, and Sir William, who commanded her."

The town of Cezimbra lies at the bottom of a bay which affords excellent anchorage. It was then, as now, built of stone; and near it was the ancient fort or castle still named the Cavallo, strong, spacious, and then well mounted with heavy ordnance. On the summit of the hill behind it was an old priory, the situation of which, with cannon, rendered it impregnable, and able to command the town, the castle, and the roadstead. Close to the shore, and under the guns of the Cavallo, lay the rich carack, which was the object of so much warlike solicitude.

Attack on Cezimbra.

168

The eleven galleys had secured themselves beside a small neck of rock on the western part of the roads, anchored side by side, with the stems outward, to play upon the English as they entered; for each galley carried a very large cannon in her lofty beak, besides four other pieces in the prow below it; and they were secure from the fire of the English till the latter were under that of the castle and town. So advantageously were they placed that, as the captain of one of them confessed after his capture, their officers confidently expected with their great guns to sink the English easily. The latter saw vast quantities of tents pitched near the shore, and troops, as we have said, to the number of 20,000 men, under the Conde de Vitageria, were mustered there. Boats were seen passing all day long between the carack and the town. At first it was supposed the Spaniards were unloading her; but instead of this, they were filling her with men and ammunition.

At daybreak on the morning of the 3rd of June, the admiral fired a gun and ran his ensign to the mainmast-head; Sir William Monson responded by another, and displayed his colours at the foretop-mast-head, while the squadron stood in towards the point of attack. The vice-admiral was the sternmost ship; and each vessel as she entered the roadstead had to fight her guns on both sides at once, as they had to encounter the fire of the town, the castle, the galleys, and the carack.

The vice-admiral himself relates that, when he entered the action, he strove to luff up as near the shore as he could, when he came to anchor, plying both his broadsides the while; and by that time the fire of the leading ships had battered the galleys, torn up the benches, freeing in vast numbers the slaves, who were usually chained thereto, but who were now seen throwing themselves into the sea, and swimming towards the English ships.

The battle in the roadstead lasted till five o'clock in the

afternoon, and by that time the galleys were rowed from side to side of the harbour, making desperate efforts to avoid the fire of the ship of the vice-admiral, which he had anchored so skilfully that Sir Richard Levison "came on board him and openly, in the view and hearing of the whole ship's company, embraced him, and told him that he had won his heart for ever."

Levison's ship was less skilfully handled, for, by the negligence of her master, or some other cause, she failed to anchor at the place intended; and falling away to leeward, was ultimately carried by wind and tide, not only out of the action, but actually out of the harbour, and could not be brought in again till next day.

This circumstance enraged Sir Richard, who put himself on board the *Dreadnought*, and had anchored her near the vice-admiral, about two in the afternoon.

Three hours afterwards it was resolved to parley with the enemy, and orders were issued to all the ships to cease firing, till the English messenger returned. The man selected for the service was a merchant captain, named Sewell, who had escaped and swum off from the galleys (after having been four years a prisoner in one), as many other Christians and Turks did, when chance shots had freed them of their fetters; for by this time the galleys, on whose strength the defence had mainly rested, were some in flames, with their wretched crews on board, others were knocked to pieces, and had their benches covered by bloody corpses, and some had slipped their cables and fled.

Sewell was to intimate that the English had full possession of the roadstead; that the fort could not withstand their ordnance, nor the carack either, and that unless the latter was given up the Spaniards "were to expect all the cruelty and rigour that a conqueror could inflict upon his enemy."

After some conference, the officer commanding in the carack said that "he would send some gentlemen of quality on board with commission to treat, and desired that some of the same rank from the English might repair to him for the same purpose."

The Spanish cavaliers came on board the *Dreadnought*, where the admiral and Sir William Monson were awaiting the return of Captain Sewell; but they had immediately to return to the carack, on board of which an uproar had taken place, as one party there proposed to yield her up, and another wished to set her on fire. On learning this, Sir William Monson lowered himself into his barge, and instantly boarded her. When on deck, he was recognised by several Spanish gentlemen, who had known him when he was a prisoner of war among them.

The captain of the carrack was Don Diego Lobo, a hidalgo of noble birth. He came down into the waist, and between him and Sir William there followed a conference in the Portuguese language. He proposed to give up the cargo, provided he was permitted to retain the crew, with their arms, and the ship with her ordnance, and her colours flying. But these terms Sir William rejected, adding that he "would never permit a Spanish flag to be borne in presence of the queen's ships, unless it were disgracefully over the poop;" a reply the exact significance of which is not very clear in the present day, as it is there the colours are now shown on the jack-staff.

It was ultimately arranged to yield her up, and that the castle of Cezimbra should not fire on the English ships while they rode in the bay; and that night Sir William had the Captain Don Juan and many other Spanish gentlemen at supper in his cabin, where they had music, mirth, and pleasure.

In the beginning nearly of this engagement, the Portuguese galleys, under Santa Cruz, took to flight; the Spanish, under Spinola, fought bravely, on which in very shame the former returned to their stations; but had the English fleet possessed sufficient boats, they had all been taken or burned. One of them was named the *Leva*, in which Sir William Monson had been a prisoner in 1591, The loss of the Spaniards in the castle, carack, and galleys is unknown, but they were so full of men that it must have been considerable, while the loss of the English was most trivial - only twelve killed and wounded, chiefly on board the *Garland*. Sir William had the left wing of his doublet carried away by a,ball, from which we may infer that he did not fight in armour, The next day the squadron sailed for England, bringing with it the carack, which had wintered in the Mozambique Channel, where 600 of her crew had died of disease, and only twenty survived to see Europe; and they had suffered many calamities and misfortunes, before they unluckily came to anchor in the harbour of Cezimbra.

Carack, or *carraca*, was the name usually given by the Spaniards and Portuguese to the vessels they sent to Brazil and the Indies; they were large, round-built, and adapted, alike for; battle and burden. They were narrower above water than below, and had sometimes seven or eight decks, and were capable of carrying 2,000 tons and 2,000 men. Similar ships were used by the Knights of Rhodes and the Genoese.

The Viceroy of Portugal, Don Christoyal de Moro, was indignant and infuriated by the capture of this particular carack, under the guns of Cezim Tara, those of eleven galleys, and in the face of 20,000 troops.

He made a prisoner of Don Diego Lobo, and would have put him to death, had he not, with the aid of his sister, escaped by a window, and fled to Italy; but his patent as Governor of Malacca was confiscated, and he was reduced to penury.

Thirteen, years afterwards, in 1615, he was wandering about London, when he suddenly bethought him of Sir William Monson, who interested himself in his behalf with the Archduke and the Infanta, who restored to him his rank and property; "the poor gentleman," concludes Sir William, "being thus tossed by the waves of calamity from one country to another, and never finding likelihood of rest till now (when) Death, that masters all men, cut him short just as he was preparing his journey to Spain. And this was the end of an unfortunate and gallant young gentleman, whose deserts were worthy of a better reward, if God was pleased to afford it to him."

But Sir William Monson had not seen the last of the roads of Cezimbra. He had barely cast anchor in Plymouth Sound when he was summoned to the presence of Queen Elizabeth, who had a long conference with him, in presence of the High Admiral, her treasurer, and secretary, concerning the defence of the coast of Ireland, and certain armaments which the indefatigable Spaniards were again collecting at the Groyne; and it was resolved that he should at once sail, with what would now be called a fleet of observation, to watch that place, and not leave the coast of Spain until he saw the object of those preparations. If they proved to be simply for defence, and not invasion, he was then to join the Dutch fleet at the Rock of Lisbon. On receiving his final orders, he repaired to Plymouth, and took command of his squadron. It consisted of ten sail, as follows:- The *Swiftsure*, of 400 tons and 200 men, commanded by himself in person; *Mary Rose*, 600 tons and 250 men, Captain Trevor; *Dreadnought*, 400 tons and 200 men, Captain Cawfield; *Adventure*, 250 tons and 120 men, Captain Norris; *Answer*, 200 tons and 100 men. Captain Bredgate; *Quittance*, 200 tons and 100 men, Captain Browne; *Lion's Whelp*, 200 tons and 100 men, Captain May. With these were the *Paragon*, a merchant ship, and a small caravel.

On the 31st of August he sailed from Plymouth, and encountered much rough weather, but preferred to keep at sea rather than return. He reached the Groyne, and found the Spanish squadron had left that place, under the flag of Don Diego de Borachero, for Lisbon. He dispatched the little caravel to the Bayona Isles, a number of insular rocks at the entrance of the

Bay of Bayonne, off the Galician coast, to gather intelligence; and there she saw the Spanish fleet, consisting of twenty-four sail; and her captain learned from the crew of a boat he captured that they were on the look-out for the English.

Pursuing a ship, with the *Dreadnought*, into the roads of Cezimbra, he cannonaded the castle, and was fired on in return, and captured a caravel, but afterwards dismissed her. Sailing once more to the Rock, he could see nothing of the Dutch fleet, without a junction with which it would have been perilous, with so small a squadron, to engage the Spaniards.

On the night of the 26th September he saw a light upon the sea, and, thinking it might come from the fleet of St. Thomas or the Brazils, he gave immediate chase, and on hailing the vessels in the gloom, he suddenly found by their great size and number that he was among the armada of Don Diego, with only the *Adventure* and *Whelp* in his company, the rest of his squadron having been scattered four nights before in a storm. He compelled a Spanish prisoner to respond to the hailing of

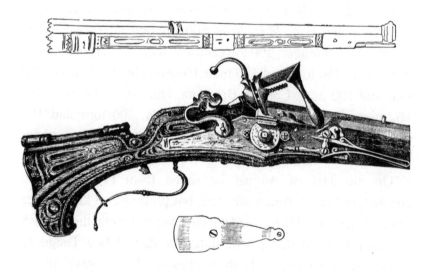

Musket of 1620, showing wheel and match combined.

his countrymen, but the wind was so high that they could not hear him.

The *Adventure* was now discovered to be an English ship; she was fired upon, and had many of her men killed and wounded; but she, with the *Dreadnought* and *Whelp*, passed right through the enemy's fleet, with their poop lanterns lighted, and when day broke they were far ahead of the Spaniards, who immediately made all sail in chase, and their leading ships soon overtook the *Whelp* and opened their guns upon her.

Then it was, as Sir William relates of himself, that, "resolving not to see even a pinnace of Her Majesty's so lost, if he could rescue her with the hazard of his life, though it was much against the persuasions of his master and company," he shortened sail and ordered the *Whelp* to lie her course, while he prepared to engage the three leading ships of the enemy.

On perceiving by this movement how reckless was the bravery of Monson, the Spanish admiral, to the astonishment of the English, fired a gun as a signal for his fleet to follow him, and sheering off, stood in shore.

Monson now bore up for the South Cape, in hope to meet the San Domingo fleet of richly-laden merchantmen, but it had escaped him by passing two days before; and on the 21st of October, descrying a great galleon of the King of Spain, he gave immediate chase to her, though she steered for shelter in shore, and at length came to anchor under the guns of the castle situated on Cape. St. Vincent, a rocky promontory, forming the most western point of Portugal and at the same time also of Europe.

His boarders were all ready with pike, and bill, and axe, but he failed to board her, "through the fear and cowardliness of the man at the helm, who bore up" when he was ready to do so; and the fight that ensued was long, sharp, and dangerous, though not a shot was exchanged till they were only the ships' length apart.

175

The castle, which was one of great strength, was playing upon Monson's ship, and its cannon so battered and rent her that he says "a team of oxen might have crept through her under the half-deck." He had seven men slain by one shot alone. He had others killed and many more wounded, as he had to encounter both the galleon and the fortress; and this unequal conflict he maintained in sight of a Spanish squadron, under Sirriago, that lay to the westward of the cape, and several English men-of-war that lingered to the eastward, but dared not attempt his rescue, "for fear of the castle."

He continued the battle till nightfall, and then, to elude the fleet that lay to the westward waiting to capture him, and to seek for belter fortune, he sailed for the island of Terceira; but when within fifty leagues of it he was long becalmed. Then, finding that provisions were failing him, and that one of his masts, which had been wounded, went overboard, with the first suitable breeze he bore up for England; and in this crippled condition reached Plymouth on the 20th of November, 1602, where he found that the *Dreadnought*, the *Adventure*, and *Mary Rose*, with nearly all their crews dead or sick, had preceded him.

Sir William Monson tells us that he was the general (by which he means admiral) of the last fleet of Queen Elizabeth, and adds that he had served her from the beginning of the Spanish wars; having, when a youth, been at the capture of the first Spanish prize that was brought into an English port, and which was taken with the loss of twenty-five men killed and fifty wounded. She was afterwards manned as a ship of war against the Spaniards, and named the *Commander*. She belonged to Sir George Carew, then Governor of the Isle of Wight.

At the death of Elizabeth her fleet consisted of forty-two sail, ranging from the *Triumph*, of 1,000 tons and 500 men, down to the *Penny Rose*, hoy, of 80 tons and 8 men, and the *Squint*, of 20 tons and 2 men, when in harbour.

- C H A P T E R   X V -

SEA-FIGHT WITH THE TURKS OFF CAGLIARI, 1617

THE YEAR 1603 saw the peaceful accession of James VI of Scotland to the English throne. This pedantic monarch had none of those qualities that distinguished his ancestors, but the union of the crowns in his person was a great benefit to the people of. Great, Britain. Never more on British soil could there be such battles as Bannockburn or Flodden, fought by rival monarchs. Nor was there need for the future to keep watch and ward along the border-side by tower and beacon; while, as subjects of the same king, the moss-troopers of both countries had to cease their raids and predatory warfare. But civil wars were to come, and Englishmen and Scotsmen were yet, unhappily, fated to meet each other in battles that were fierce and bloody, when armies had taken the form of divisions and brigades, regiments and companies, according to the tactics of the present time.

On the 12th of April, 1606, the Union Jack - the flag that has waved in so many bloody and victorious battles by sea and shore - first made its appearance. From Rymer's "Fœdera," and the Annals of Sir James Balfour, Lord Lyon King at Arms, we learn that some differences having arisen between ships of the two countries at sea, His Majesty ordained that a *new flag* be adopted, with the crosses of St. Andrew and St George interlaced, by placing the latter fimbriated on the blue flag of Scotland as the ground thereof. This flag all ships were to carry at their main-top; but English ships were to display St. George's red cross at their stern, and the Scottish the white saltire of St. Andrew. The Union Jack, however, was not adopted by the troops of either country till their Parliamentary union, in 1707.

In Munro's account of the expedition with Mackay's regiment in Denmark, he states that in 1626 the Scots in the Danish army persisted in carrying their national flag, and refused to place the Danish cross upon it.

The arms and armour of the time of James were little more than a continuation of those of Elizabeth; but the increasing use of fire-arms, and the improvements thereon, brought mail more into disrepute, so that by the close of his reign that of the heaviest cavalry terminated at the knees. In Drayton's "Polyolbion," Henry Prince of Wales appears in armour only to the waist, with a plumed and visored basinet beside him, and steel gauntlets on his hands. The armour of Sir Horace Vere, a plain suit in the Tower, is, however, complete from head to heel, and is about the date" of 1606.

It was now begun to be found that good buff leather would, of itself, resist the cut of a sword, and was thus adopted as the dress for lightly-armed cavalry; so armour was now beginning" to terminate "in the same materials with which it began - the skins of animals, or leather" (Grose's "Military Antiquities").

To the rest for the musket or matchlock, there was added to the equipment of the musketeer in the time of James a long blade, for his defence after he had fired. This was called a Swedish feather, or "hog's bristle." It was originally a Swedish invention, and was put by the musketeer to the same use that the English archers were wont to put their pointed stakes in the days of Cressy and Agincourt.

In this reign we first read of the simple military mourning which is in use to the present day. Colonel Munro, in his "Expedition," mentions that when Captain Learmonth, of Mackay's Highlanders, died of his wounds at Hamburg, in 1627, "for his sake, and in remembrance of his worth and valour, the whole officers of the regiment did wear a black mourning ribband."

Save the expedition under Sir Robert Mansell to Algiers - an abortive affair, which covered the Government with ridicule - no warlike event of importance marked the reign of the peaceful and pedantic James I of Great Britain; though there occurred a sea-fight off the Isle of Sardinia, between one English merchant ship and no less than six Turkish men-of-war, which made much noise, in the year 1616.

Two accounts of this spirited battle were published: one by the English captain, in the following year, and dedicated to Henry Stuart, the young Prince of Wales; and the other by John Taylor, the "water poet," an author now little known, though a note to the "Dunciad" states that "he wrote fourscore books in the reigns of James and Charles I."

Towards the close of December, 1616, the ship *Dolphin*, of London, Captain Edward Nicholls, left Zante, one of the Ionian

Musketeer   *Pikeman*
(From an Undated Tract, "Exercise of the English Militia" - about 1625.)

Isles, with a full cargo for the Thames. She was a craft of 220 tons, or thereabout; her crew consisted of thirty-six men and two boys; and she was armed with nineteen pieces of cast ordnance and five "murderers," a name then given to small pieces of cannon having chambers, and made to load at the breech. They were mostly used at sea, in order to clear the decks when an enemy had boarded a vessel. Her master was "a man of great skill, courage, industry, and proved experience;" and these good qualities were soon to be put to a terrible test.

On the 1st of January, 1617, the *Dolphin* lost sight of the Fior de Levante, and on the morning of the 8th sighted the island of Sardinia. The wind being westerly, at nine in the morning she stood in shore for Cagliari, and about noon was close to two small watchtowers, from which two cannon were fired, as a signal that the guards there wished to speak with the crew. Their object, Captain Nicholls afterwards learned, was to acquaint him that Turkish war-vessels were cruising off the coast; but their intention was misunderstood, and the *Dolphin's* course was continued towards the Cabo di Paula, westward of the Gulf of Cagliari.

On the 12th of January, at four o'clock in the morning watch, they discovered, with doubt and alarm, a large ship steering towards them. She proved to be a sattie, or Turkish craft, which Captain Nicholls describes as being "much like unto an argosy, of a very great burthen and bigness," and manned by armed men. Perceiving that she was endeavouring to get between the *Dolphin* and the island of Sardinia, the master sent a seaman into the maintop "with his perspective glass," from where he saw five other vessels coming up before a south-west breeze.

"He perceived them to be Turkish men-of-war, the first of them booming by himself before the wind, with his flag in the maintop and his sails gallantly spread abroad. After him came the admiral and vice-admiral, of greater burden than the first;

after him two more - the rear-admiral, larger than ail the rest, and his companion."

Their ports were open, and it was evident they were bent on hostility and mischief; so the *Dolphin* cleared away for action. Powder and shot were served out for the guns; the crew armed themselves and stood to their quarters, while the captain harangued them in the following terms from the poop:-

"Countrymen and fellows! You see into what an exigency it has pleased God to suffer us to fall. Let us remember that we are but men, and must of necessity die, where, when, and how, is of God's appointment; but if it be His pleasure that this must be the last of our days, His will be done; and let us, for His glory, our souls' welfare, our country's honour, and the credit of ourselves, fight valiantly to the last gasp ! Let us prefer a noble death to a life of slavery; and if we die, let us die to gain a. better life !"

He then assured those who might survive that, if maimed, they should be maintained as long as they lived, and be secured from want, adding, "Be therefore resolute, and stand to it, for here there is no shrinking. We must be either free men 01 slaves. Die with me, or if you will not, by God's grace, I shall die with you!"

He brandished his sword; the crew responded by loud cheers, and the trumpets were sounded, as he was assailed in succession by the sattie and the five other Turkish ships, the size and strength of which vary in the two accounts, but are given thus by Captain Schomberg in his "Naval Chronology:"Two of 300 tons, 28 guns, and 250 men each; one of 200 tons, 24 guns, and 250 men; two of 200 tons, 22 guns, and 200 men each. In the sattie were said to be 1,500 men.

The leading Turkish ship got to windward of the *Dolphin*, one of whose crew was killed by the first shot from her; and in the fight that ensued, her heavy guns so battered and beat down the bulwarks of the *Dolphin* "that," says Nicholls, "we used our guns clear of the ports," as she was all exposed and open. But so bravely fought the crew of the little English ship, that the ordnance of the Turk was dismounted, nearly half her crew were slain, and the officers were seen beating the others with their scimitars to keep them to their duty. Moreover, the *Dolphin* had given her many dangerous shots between wind and water.

By this time she was laid aboard by the 200-ton ship, the captain of which proved to be an English renegade, named Walsingham. He fought his way over her larboard quarter at the head of a gang of ferocious desperadoes, armed with sabres ("which were called faulchions"), hatchets, and half-pikes. The conflict on the poop continued for half an hour, during which the Turks strove to tear up the "nail-board and trap-hatch j "but the well-directed fire from a murderer in the round-house abaft the mainmast swept them away and cleared that portion of the ship; while theirs was plied by cannon, musketry, and another murderer, that was planted in the trap-hatch, till her hull was shot through and through. She fell away astern, receiving a parting broadside as she passed, and lay to, that her leaks and shot-holes might be plugged; and this ended "Walsingham's part in the fight," which the Sardinians on the shore gathered in numbers to see.

And now the shattered *Dolphin* was assailed by two other Turks, of 300 tons each, one of which was commanded by another renegade, named Kelly, probably an Irishman, who carried his flag in the maintop, while the other's ensign was hoisted at the fore. Ranging close alongside, one boarded her on the starboard quarter, the other on the larboard, or, as it is now called, port side. They poured in "thick and threefold, with their scimitars, hatchets, half-pikes, and other weapons," and with loud shouts and yells of fury and defiance. They succeeded in tearing down the British flag; but the steward of the *Dolphin* shot the Turk who had it, and he was flung into the sea, while the flag remained on deck. After a conflict maintained for an hour and a half, by sweeping the deck with the murderers, and the vigorous use of their weapons, the ship was again cleared, and the Turks were compelled "to lay their ships by to stop their leaks, for they had been grievously torn and battered;" but the *Dolphin* was not yet free, for she was almost immediately assailed by "two more of Captain Kelly's ships."

But notwithstanding this overwhelming force, that the *Dolphin's* crew was lessened by death, and that nearly all who were left to fight did so covered with wounds and blood, "we shot them quite through and through," says Nicholls, "and laid him likewise by the lee, as we had done the others before." But they were boarded again by the other ship, on the starboard quarter, and summoned to yield, with promises of quarter, liberty, and half the cargo. To these offers no attention was paid; by pike and sword they were all tumbled overboard, and the ship again cleared, but ere this was achieved the *Dolphin* caught fire, balls of burning matter being tossed into her by the enemy. One of these lighted in the basin of the surgeon, as he was in the act of dressing the wounds of the master, who, though injured in both legs, had still to stand by the tiller, and steer.

The fire was extinguished, and the sorely-battered *Dolphin* crept in shore, and was about to anchor, when another ship bore down to attack her.

Her appearance so alarmed Nicholls, that he slipped or cut his cable and ran into the roadstead of Cagliari, and took shelter between the two forts whose signals he had some time before disregarded. There he remained for five days repairing damages, attending to the wounded, and burying the dead on shore; for, after all this boarding and cannonading, his loss was only seventeen killed, but all the survivors were more ox less injured.

These Turks were doubtless corsairs; as Nicholls says that three of their captains were Englishmen, who came "to rob and spoil upon the ocean, and their names were Walsingham, Kelly, and Sampson. After encountering a dreadful tempest, during which one of her wounded men died and was cast overboard, in the middle of February the *Dolphin* came safely to anchor in the Thames.

THE ISLE OF RHÉ, 1627

T O ADD to the difficulties in which the year 1626 found Charles I involved at home and abroad, a war was declared with France, and of that war his favourite, the unpopular Duke of Buckingham, was the cause. Bold, presumptuous, and amorous, when employed to bring over the Princess Henrietta, the bride of Charles I, he is said to have paid his addresses to the Queen of France, Anne of Austria, whose nature was as warm as his own. Hence he projected a new embassy to France, which Cardinal Richelieu prevented, by making Louis send a message to the effect that he must not think of such a journey; but Buckingham, in the heat of his romantic passion, swore, says Clarendon, that "he would see the queen in spite of all the power of France!" From that moment he determined to engage Britain in a war with that kingdom.

He procured the dismissal, of Queen Henrietta's French attendants, contrary to her marriage treaty; he encouraged the seizure of French ships by English, men-of-war and privateers; but finding that these injuries produced only 'remonstrances and embassies, he resolved to second the intrigues of the Duc de Soubize, by a military expedition into France, to succour Rochelle, a Huguenot city, the capture and suppression of which was one of the grand objects of the cardinal's government, and his troops were then besieging it. "This Englishman," says Voltaire, "made his master declare war against France merely because that Court had refused him the liberty of carrying on his amour. Such an adventure seemed more adapted to the times of Amadis de Gaul; but so connected and interwoven are the affairs of this world, that the romantic amours of the Duke of Buckingham produced a religious war and the taking of Rochelle!"

Charles had but small sympathy, perhaps, with the Huguenots, who so much resembled his own sour Puritans in discipline and worship, in politics and religion; but he allowed himself to be won over by the arguments of Soubize, the Huguenot leader, then in London, and by the ardent solicitations of Buckingham: thus an armament was prepared by land and sea for the relief of Rochelle.

Buckingham, says the Jesuit, Père d'Orleans, believed that a war against France, in favour of a Protestant faction, was an enterprise so much to the taste of the nation that, though hated by the English Parliament, he never imagined that body would obstruct him; but he was somewhat deceived, as the event proved.

There was fitted for sea a fleet composed of forty-two men-of-war and twenty-three transports, having on board seven regiments of a thousand men each, a squadron of horse, and many French Protestant refugees; and it was given out that this force was destined for the recovery of the Palatinate. By

Cagliari, from the sea.

The Duke of Buckingham's army at the Isle of Rhé.

a Royal Commission, the duke was made Admiral of the Fleet and Commander of the Land Forces, among which Sir James Balfour states there were 3,000 Scots, commanded by William, Earl of Morton, K.G., and captain of the King's Guard.

By this time, military training had become more and more the study of the soldier. In a treatise called "England's Trainings," published in 1619, by Edward Davis, we find the mode of handling the matchlock by the English musketeer.

"A soldier must either, accustom himself to bear a piece or a pike. If he bear a piece, then must he first learn to hold the same, to accommodate his match between the two foremost fingers and his thumb, and to plant the great end on his breast with a gallant soldier-like grace; and if ignorant, to the intent that he may be more encouraged, let him acquaint himself first with the firing of touch-powder in his panne, and so by degrees both to shoot off, to bow and bear up his bodye, and so, consequently, to attain to the level and practice of an assured and serviceable shot, readily to charge and, with a comely touch, discharge, making sure at the same instant of his mark, with a quick and vigilant eie."

This process is precisely the same as the snapping and aiming drill of the present hour. Davis adds, "His flaske and touch-box must keep his powder, his purse and mouth his bullets; in skirmish his left hand must hold his match and piece, and the right hand use the office of charging and discharging."

A most complete detail of the then elaborate system of drilling pikemen and musketeers, in the first years of Charles's reign, will be found in a quaint folio volume of the Scottish Colonel Munro, published at London, in 1637, by "William Jones, in Red Crosse Street." Platoon firing was first practised by the Scottish troops; and Harte says, in his "Life of Gustavus Adolphus," that by this new method they spread terror and amazement among the Austrians in the wars of Germany.

The musketeers, says Munro, should be formed in companies with a front of thirty-two men, but six ranks deep; the first, firing at once, casting about and reloading; the second rank passing to the front between the files, to give fire next; then the third rank, and so on; "all blowing, priming, casting about, and charging all alike, where they stand, till *per vices* the whole ranckes have discharged, till the enemye turn back, or that they come to push of pike." About this period, the *rondelle*, or *rondache*, as the French called it, a light shield or target, was pretty generally used by the pikeman. A good example of one of these is still preserved at Warwick Castle.

Rondelle, Warwick Castle, 1620.

The English would seem to have early adopted a steady rate of marching, but less quick than the French. An old author of 1630, writing on this subject, says, "I remember to have heard say that upon a time the old Marshal Biron bid Sir Roger Williams bring up his companies faster, taxing the slow march of the English. ' Sir,' said he, ' with this march our forefathers conquered, your country of France, and I mean not to alter it!' - a memorable answer of an honourable soldier" ("Relations of the Most Famous Kingdoms").

Buckingham's armament sailed from Portsmouth on the 7th of June, 1627, leaving eleven sail, which were not quite ready for sea, to follow him; but they were off the Isle of Rhé before him, as the fleet had spent some time in pursuit of certain Dunkirkers. On seeing the English' ships, the Rochellers shut their gates to the seaward, fearing some snare or surprise, as they had no tidings given to them previously that relief was coming from England.

On the 12th of July, the duke sent Soubize and Sir William Beecher to the city with a message, and they were admitted by a small postern gate, to deliver it to the Huguenot leaders. It was to the effect that "the King of England, out of compassion for their sufferings, had sent a fleet and army to their assistance; and if they refused his aid, he declared that he was fully quit of his engagement of honour and conscience for their relief."

The mayor replied, in the name of the inhabitants, that "they most humbly thanked His Majesty for the care he had of them; but that, being in strict union with all the Protestants of France, they could not receive into the city the offered succours without consulting their friends, and obtaining previously the consent of the whole body of Huguenots."

By this reply, the duke finding himself shut out of Rochelle, directed his course to the Isle of Rhé, where the officer commanding the French troops was the Marquis de Thoiras, afterwards a Marshal of France, whom Sir Philip Warwick, in his Memoirs, calls an old and well-experienced soldier, who had in readiness such a force as made the intention of the British alike hazardous and dangerous. The duke's first blunder, in appearing unannounced and unexpectedly before Rochelle, was now to be followed by another; for, instead of attacking the fertile and defenceless Isle of Oleron, he turned his attention to that of Rhé, which was both well-garrisoned and strongly fortified. It lies opposite to Rochelle, is of irregular form, about eighteen miles long by three broad. Its capital, St. Martin, was defended by a citadel, and on the shore were several forts.

The mode of landing was arranged by a council of colonels, and the event took place at four o'clock in the afternoon of the 12th, near La Prée, a fort with which some shots were exchanged. The *Rainbow*, the *Vanguard*, and two other ships, under Robert, Earl of Lindsay, who was Admiral of England and Governor of Berwick, were to lie well in shore, near a promontory, while the *Globe*, the *Lion*, and the *Chameleon* came to anchor near the islet of St. Martin; all their sides to be lined with musketeers, to scour the beach while the boats went off.

The army was formed in three divisions, and, when landed, the different regiments were to be formed in contiguous battalions, one hundred yards apart; each soldier to have powder, shot, and provisions for two days; a quartermaster to follow each regiment with ammunition alone. The landing was accordingly effected in this fashion, but not without disorder, as there was a scarcity of boats, and they were fired on by the enemy.

Buckingham had only got ashore 1500 men, with four small pieces of cannon, called drakes, under Sir John Burroughs, Sir Alexander Bret, Sir Charles Conway, and others, when 200 French cavalry, who had been concealed in a hollow, made a furious charge, and "put our men, being un-ranked," to the rout, driving many into the sea, where they were drowned.

By the example of the duke, Sir William Heydon, Sir Thomas York, and other officers, this disordered party faced about and began firing. They thus repulsed the cavalry, who fell back, with the loss of 120 men, on a body of infantry, whose officers led them on, waving their plumed hats and brandishing their swords. But, after a few volleys of shot, on the advance of the pikemen, now formed in close ranks, they were put to flight, but not until the British had some eighty soldiers drowned and twenty slain, together with no less than thirty officers killed and wounded. Among the former were Sir William Heydon, General of the Ordnance; Sir Thomas York, Quartermaster-General; Sir Thomas Thornhurst, Lieutenant-Colonel; eight captains, including Wodehouse, Corporal of the Field; Johnson, an engineer; Netherton, a quartermaster; three lieutenants, two ensigns, and a sergeant.

That night Buckingham got the cavalry squadron ashore, and threw up a trench, as another attack was expected; but none was made, as some discussion or difference of opinion as to the mode of defence had taken place between the Marquis de Thoiras and the Baron de St. Andre, who resented the marquis having assigned to his brother the honour of first attacking the invaders, who had actually defeated the Regiment of Champagne, in whose ranks were many men of the best families in France, and which had been first embodied by Henry II in 1558, and had ever boasted of its stainless reputation in war; and Buckingham committed a third blunder in not instantly following up the repulse of that corps, which fell back in such disorder that he might with tolerable ease have made himself master of St. Martin.

Next morning a French trumpeter came from De Thoiras with a page, to ask if Buckingham meant "to give him a breakfast."' The duke sent them back with twenty-five pieces of silver. He still did not despair of getting quietly into Rochelle, as a message came thence to the effect, says Greenville, that they could show no countenance to the English till the Isle of Rhé" was cleared, and until they got' in their wine and coal. The Marquis de Thoiras, who was rapidly strengthening all his posts, now sent another trumpeter concerning the burial of the French dead, offering-great ransoms for some of the slain who were of high rank, and who were carried out of the English entrenchments and delivered to the French in carts. The duke was now joined by Soubize, with 500 French Huguenot gentlemen from Rochelle; and the troops marched out of the trenches a few bowshots to the front, but retired again to their bivouac.

Buckingham now passed days in unmeaning delays. He allowed the wary old soldier, De Thoiras, to amuse him with deceitful negotiations, while he was strengthening St. Martin's to stand a siege; and he was so negligent in guarding the sea by his shipping that he permitted a strong French force to steal into the island in small divisions.

He marched to La Flotte, a little town, where he halted for the night, and next day appeared before the town of St. Martin's, where a Scottish officer, named Sir William Cunningham (says Sanderson, in his " History of Charles I"), "dared any to single combate;" but the town was abandoned by 400 men, who left twenty pieces of cannon behind them.

Buckingham had promised King Charles that he would reduce the citadel of St. Martin in eight days; yet he was detained before it by De Thoiras till the month of November, for to the old works on the place were now added many new.

Sanderson describes it as being quadrangular, with sloping parapets, and four great bastions, or bulwarks, named after the king, queen, Thoiras, and Antioch. In these were galleries loopholed for musketry, and on their summits were fascines and hurdles of baskets and earth. The trenches, which were of great depth, could be filled with water. It was further defended by other works in the form of half-moons and ravelins, over which the great guns of the central tower could play with ease.

On the 20th the duke had a battery erected against the citadel, while he left the regiments of Sir Peregrine Bertie and Sir Henry Sprye with the cavalry at La Flotte, to cover or secure a retreat if such became necessary; and there Sir William Heydon, who died, was buried in the Protestant churchyard, "with a soldier's peal - three or four brave volleys of shot."

The siege was now pressed with considerable vigour. Some windmills near the citadel were stormed and burned, and thirty French musketeers who were in them captured. The fire of the battery damaged the citadel but little, while the guns of the latter slew many of the duke's men, who were much exposed.

Passing the French army before Rochelle at the hazard of his life, Mr. George Monk (the Albemarle of a future time) reached the Island of Rhé" from England, with tidings of French preparations by land and sea. The barge of the *Triumph* captured a boatful of men and provisions, bound for the citadel, and her crew put all to the sword save three, who were "commanders of quality," and one of whom is styled as standard-bearer to the King of France. Two other boats were sunk with all on board.

On the 8th of August the British trenches were scoured by a party of horse from the citadel, but many of these were slain as they retired. A few days after, to push the siege, 500 seamen were brought from the fleet under a Captain Weddel, who received the rank of colonel, for which we are told he was "laughed out of employment by the landsmen." Buckingham's anxiety to have the place reduced by famine or assault increased daily, as the gathering armaments of France would soon swallow up his little force. Cardinal Richelieu obtained ships from Havre de Grâce, and from Spain; among these were thirty large frigates. All were filled with armed men; and the services of Pompeo de

Farago, a famous engineer of Dunkirk, were to be employed, for the destruction of the English fleet by fire.

On the duke being joined by some Irish auxiliaries, under Sir Ralph Bingley and Sir Piers Crosby, the council of colonels became anxious for more active measures than mere cannonading; but delays, caused by parleys on various pretences - all the scheme of Thoiras to gain time - ensued with the consent of Buckingham, who rapidly lost favour with the troops.

An assault, before a breach had been effected, was made on the 23rd of September, when the prospects of starvation or being cut off made the troops doubly desperate; but they were over-matched by the regiment of Champagne. From the ramparts fully a hundred of the British were killed by stones alone; mines were sprung, and the stormers were repulsed with a loss of more than 400 men, and many prisoners, thirty of whom were taken "in traps which they had made in their trenches."

French troops were now pouring into the island every night - on one occasion 1,000 men landed from twenty boats in the face of the fleet - and a retreat or abandonment of the enterprise was urged upon Buckingham by Sir Edward Hawley and Sergeant-Major Brett, in the name of the Military Council; but he declined, until some of Sir William Cunningham's cavalry, who had been scouting, came in to report that they heard the sound of heavy firing on the mainland.

By that time Count Schomberg was on the island, with 7,000 of the finest infantry of France, including the Royal Guard, and the regiments of Navarre and Piedmont, and had possessed himself of La Prée, a fort which the duke had overlooked; and now, with an army decimated by disease, exposure, and starvation, rather than by the casualties of war, he consented to retreat, and the movement was executed so unskilfully that it became a fatal rout.

The garrisoning of La Prée and other forts on the isle left him

195

no other point for embarkation than the Isle de l'Oye, which is separated from Rhé by salt-pits and a channel, through which lay a long and narrow causeway. Followed closely by the French, the British began to retire, but were not much molested until they began to cross the causeway to reach the boats of the fleet, and then they were furiously charged by the French, among whom was a body of cavalry, and a dreadful scene of confusion and slaughter ensued as the rear was driven in disorder upon the centre and front.

Five men only could pass abreast. The English, under Brett and Rich, and the Scots, under the Earl of Morton (who was labouring like the other two under a severe illness), had begun to defile across with four pieces of cannon, while some other troops, under Courtenay, Hawley, and Bingley, strove to keep a front to the enemy, but in vain; the army became "like a body without a head," to quote "Strafford's Letters," Vol. I., "like a flock without a shepherd. The French falling upon their rear, killed and took prisoners as they would themselves, helped by our own horse, who, to save themselves, broke, rode over our men, and put all in disorder, which made way for the slaughter They even disbanded, and shifted, there being no word of command given for the making them face about for repulsing of the enemy."

The Lord Mountjoy was taken prisoner, and received quarter; but Sir William Cunningham, who disdained to surrender, was killed. Vast numbers were drowned on each side of the causeway, others perished miserably by falling into the salt-pits. Sir William Courtenay, "a heavy, dull, covetous, old man, who had been above thirty years a private captain in Holland," fell into one of these, but was saved by one of his soldiers, who next fell in and perished unaided. Sir Piers Crosby, with 800 Irish pikemen, and Sir Thomas Fryar, with a few musketeers, alone made any attempt to cover the flight, and enable the remnant of the survivors to get on board; and, to do him justice, the Duke of Buckingham was the last man who left that fatal island, where, of the 7,000 men he brought from Britain, no less than 5,000 perished. "It was rumoured, however, in England," says Rapin, "that not above 1,500 were lost; and some even say the king was made to believe it." Fifty officers were killed between the time of landing and the retreat from the Isle of Rhé.

"Since England was England it never received so dishonourable a blow. Four colonels lost; thirty-two colours in the enemy's possession (but more lost); God knows how many men slain - they, say not above two thousand of our side, and I think not one of the enemy" ("Strafford's Letters").

The colours were taken to Paris, and hung up as trophies in Notre Dame.

The Duc de Rohan, who had taken arms as soon as the English fleet appeared off the coast of France, soon discovered the dangerous tendencies of the Huguenots, without being able

Retreat of the British from Rhé.

to do much mischief. The Rochellers, who had been at last induced to join the English on the Isle of Rhé, by sending them small supplies of food, and 500 men under the Duc de Soubize, only hastened the vengeance of the king, their master, who came in person with the great cardinal. With their provisions exhausted, they were left to endure a long and terrible siege, during which a famine ensued among them. Dogs, cats, horses, hides, and leather were devoured; and of 15,000 persons, only some 4,000 were surviving when Rochelle surrendered.

Such were the fruits of Buckingham's rash and most ill-conducted expedition to the coast of France.

He proposed a second attempt, and for this purpose the survivors of the Scottish and Irish contingents were billeted about Portsmouth, "in the country villages, to the great regret of their hosts, that had never felt any such burden before," as Sanderson expresses it; and Sir William Balfour, a Scottish commander of horse in the Netherlands, afterwards Governor of the Tower of London, received £30,000 to purchase cavalry horses for the king's service; but the enterprise, so far as the duke was concerned, was ended by the dagger of Felton, a lieutenant who had been dismissed from the service.

The result of the expedition to the Isle of Rhé had raised many complaints and loud murmurs against the duke, who had many enemies - so many had perished there, and among others, Major-General Sir John Boroughs, one of the best officers in England. And these misfortunes were universally imputed to Buckingham's incapacity, as he had never served in any war either by land or sea, and yet he had been commissioned in the double capacity of Admiral of the Fleet and Captain-General of the Army. To these complaints were added others. The seamen urged that they had been without wages for three years past; so they deserted in vast numbers, as they were determined to serve no longer without reward.

The king's ships at this time were divided into six different rates or classes, in which the pay of the officers and men varied considerably. Thus, the monthly pay of the captain of a first-rate was £14; but of a sixth rate, only £4 6s 8d.; while the seamen in all classes had 15s. without distinction; and all surgeons had £1 10s. per month, but were rated below the ship's steward and cook, who received £1 5s. (Lediard).

Troubles were "now fated to come thick and fast on England, on Scotland, and on their king; and thus a few explanations are necessary as we draw near the battles of the great Civil War.

From 1629 to 1640, a period of eleven years, no Parliament was called (except in Scotland, in 1633), a case without parallel in English history. Archbishop Laud and the Earl of Strafford were during these years the principal ministers and dangerous advisers of Charles I. As Thomas Wentworth, the earl had been a leading man among those who forced the king to ratify the Petition of Rights; but the hope of being as necessary to Charles as the more able Richelieu was to the French monarch led him to seek the Royal favour. He laid a deep scheme to undermine the strength of the House of Commons, and to secure for Charles an absolute power. This scheme he called in his private letters, "thorough," a name that well expresses its dangerous nature.

A standing army was to be raised; and though such an element in government had existed in France since the time when Charles VII established a standing force consisting of 16,000 infantry and 9,000 cavalry, divided into fifteen *compagnies d'ordonnance* (according to Père Daniel), it was unknown in England, and before it all other power in the State was to be swept away. As Viceroy of Ireland, Strafford had tried the experiment in that island in 1631, and for seven years he kept the natives and the English colonists alike cowering beneath his iron sway. Archbishop Laud conducted the affairs of the

Church; and, having very high ecclesiastical ideas of pomp and power, he viewed with rancorous bitterness the religious services of the English Puritans, and still more those of the Scottish Presbyterians.

Now all England groaned under three most irresponsible and tyrannical tribunals, conducted by these two ministers. In the Star Chamber, men were fined, imprisoned, and often cruelly mutilated, for resisting their policy. The High Commission Court launched its thunders against all who dared to differ in religious views from Laud, some of whose opinions were very peculiar; and, directed by Wentworth, a Council of York sat in that city, endowed with absolute control over all the northern counties of England.

And now, when the murmurs and discontents of the people of that country were increasing fast, Charles fired the train that was to end in his own destruction, by interfering with the Scots, who, under their own government and Parliament, had hitherto been beyond his influence. He created thirteen bishops in the Church of Scotland, and appointed a service-book to be read by the clergy; but when the Dean of St. Giles's, at Edinburgh, began to read the new liturgy, such a riot ensued that he and the bishop fled in fear. An order came from the king to enforce the new prayers by the aid of troops if necessary, as Laud was determined that Episcopacy should be the form of religion over all Britain; but the stubborn spirit of the Scots was roused, and between the months of February and March, 1638, nineteen-twentieths of the nation had signed a document in every parish church, called the National Covenant, by which they bound themselves, at the risk of life and goods, to oppose all interference in Church matters, and to unite for the defence of their laws, their freedom, and their king.

Thus in thirty short days was undone the work of thirty years, begun by James VI; and Scotland became more Presbyterian than ever. By the General Assembly, prelacy was abolished and the bishops excommunicated. Gladly would Charles and his two fatal ministers have crushed this stern opposition; but their want of money entangled them in new difficulties daily. In 1640 they were compelled to call the Short Parliament, but being met by demands with which Charles would not comply, it was dissolved; and ere the king and his minister knew very well what to do, though preparing to invade Scotland, tidings came that the Scottish army had crossed the Tweed, and was marching on Newcastle - acts of hostility which came to pass as we shall presently describe, and which Charles and the English had drawn upon themselves.

- C H A P T E R   X V I I   -
THE ROUT AT NEWBURN FORD, 1640

THE ADHERENCE of the Scots to their own form of religion so highly incensed Charles that he seized all the Scottish shipping in English ports; while Laud had the imprudence to mock and jeer in the Royal presence those Commissioners whom the Scots had sent to expostulate with the king, though already shots had been exchanged between the Covenanters and a Royalist governor, who refused to give up the regalia, which were in Edinburgh, and which the Scottish Parliament demanded. In consequence of the growing discontents of the English people, the warlike preparations made by Charles were of a less extensive nature than those of the Scots. The king, disappointed by his Parliament in his preparations for an expedition against the Scots, was compelled to have recourse to measures that were repugnant to himself. On his evil mentors, the bishops, he laid a heavy hand; but his loyal English courtiers and ministry - the cavalier faction, who sincerely loved him - contributed a loan which exceeded all his expectations. In a few days they placed £300,000 in his hands, thus enabling him to provision and garrison Berwick, Carlisle, and Newcastle; while his army, consisting of 19,000 infantry and 2,000 cavalry, began its march from York for the North. The Earl of Northumberland was Commander-in-Chief, the Earl of Strafford was Lieutenant-General, and Lord Conway, who had served at the Isle of Rhé, was General of the Horse. The Lord High Admiral of England equipped twenty sail, in addition to those furnished by the city of London; and, with a severity that Charles did not desire, the orders for ship-money were renewed by his English Ministry.

The companies of infantry then consisted of one captain, one lieutenant, one ensign, three sergeants, three corporals, three drummers, and 188 rank and file, whose aggregate pay amounted to £7 8s. 10d. per diem.

All the horses, artillery, and stores destined for the invasion of Scotland were conveyed to the great magazine and rendezvous at Newcastle, a circumstance which made the Scottish leader resolve to march on that point forthwith.

On hearing that the king was actually coming against them at the head of an army, the Scottish Parliament resolved to anticipate him, and took their measures with wonderful celerity. Stores, arms, and horses were rapidly collected; a number of 24- and 32-pounder guns were brought from Holland; the gun and shot forges at Edinburgh were put in full operation; and from the pulpits of more than a thousand parish churches, the clergy urged the people to the field.

Sir Alexander Leslie, of Balgonie, lately a Field Marshal under Gustavus Adolphus, was commissioned to act as general of the forces that were then "in arms for the defence of the Covenant for religion, crown, and country." Lord Livingstone, of Almond, was appointed Lieutenant-General; and William Baillie, lately a colonel of Dutch troops, was Major-General. Sir Alexander Hamilton, of Priestfield, was Commander of the Artillery; and Durie, of that ilk, was Commissary-General. Five earls and five lords were among the colonels of regiments composed of the usual number of pike-men, halberdiers, and musketeers. Every troop of horse and company of foot carried a standard; and, by order of the Parliament, every company was to consist of 200 men; but some were under that number. Sir James Balfour states that "there were 200 foot companies, 4,000 horse, and 2,500 bag-gagers." In this Scottish army there was one company of Irishmen, brought over by Captain Fulk Ellis from Carrickfergus.

"Many of the horse were armed with lances, in addition to their swords and pistols; the dragoons had buff coats with large skirts, sword, pistol, and slung musketoon. All the horse wore back and breast plates; to these the pikemen usually added tassettes; but there was scarcely a helmet worn in the whole Scottish army, for, by order of the nobles, the Lowland bonnet, with a knot of blue ribbons above the left ear, was worn by all ranks in the horse, foot, and artillery, thus imparting a uniform and national aspect to the force, whose march is yet preserved in the old song, 'All the Blue Bonnets are Bound for the Border.' But, amid much of real chivalry and pure enthusiasm, cant and bigotry were beginning to find their way. 'It was refreshful,' says Livingstone, the chaplain of a regiment, 'to remark that after we came to our quarters for a night, there was nothing to be heard through the whole army but singing of psalms, prayer, and reading of Scripture by the soldiers in their tents' ("Memoirs of Montrose," London, 1858).

The experience of the Scoto-Swedish officers, who brought back with them all the tactics and inventions of Gustavus, introduced great improvements into the army of the Covenant. The old pike, six ells in length, was reduced to one of fourteen feet; the ammunition, which had hitherto been carried in flasks and bandoleers, was now made up in ball-cartridges and carried in leather pouches. The regiments were formed in regular brigades. In the line of battle the pikes formed the centre of every corps, flanked by the musketeers; and Leslie, who had seen the great superiority of the Scottish infantry at Leipzig, where they formed the van and reserve of the Swedish army, contented himself with 4,000 cavalry, but that number was afterwards increased.

The Scots quitted their camp at Choice Lee, and on the 17th of August, 1640, began their march towards Coldstream; and though the English fleet blocked up a few of the Scottish ports, General Leslie left all quiet in his rear.

Five days after the King's Council, consisting of three, Laud, Hamilton, and Strafford, very unwisely denounced the whole Scottish nation, with its Parliament, Officers of State, separate institutions, and army, as "rebels and seditious subverters of the monarchy," whom it concerned the king's honour to reduce by the sword; and prayers were put up in all the churches of England, as Sanderson records, "imploring the Eternal and Merciful God, by whom kings alone reign, to bless Charles with honour and good success, especially against those traitorous subjects who, having cast off all obedience to their anointed sovereign, do at this time in a rebellious manner seek to invade this realm."

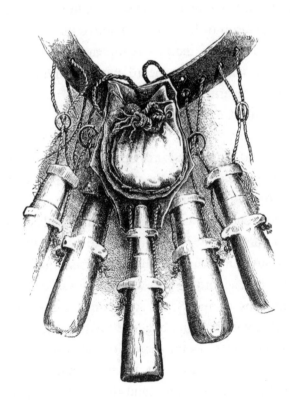

Collar of bandoleers, with cords, rings, bullet-bag, and primer

The Scottish army, finding the Tweed considerably swollen, had to halt twenty-four hours for its subsidence on the 20th, when, according to an old custom of the Scottish officers in the German wars, the colonels decided, by throwing dice on a drumhead, who should lead the van, and have the honour of treading first on the hostile ground. The lot fell on James, Earl of Montrose, the future marquis, of gallant but unfortunate memory, who rode through the river to show that it was fordable, and, waving his sword, returned to lead over his regiment of Perthshire men. Then the whole army began to cross, each colonel of infantry dismounting and fording on foot at the head of his battalion. One of the Perthshire regiment was drowned, as the water rose above their sword-belts; so, to break the force of the current, while the rear brigades and artillery crossed, Leslie formed a squadron of horse in line above the ford. It was four in the afternoon when the first regiment crossed; but the bells of the English villages were heard chiming midnight before the rear-guard of the army had passed.

By this time Charles, at the head of a mutinous and very discontented army, was marching with all speed towards Newcastle; and, trusting Lord Conway's column of English troops would at least secure the passage of the Tyne, he was not under much apprehension.

The Scots encamped on Cornhill, and repulsed: a party of horse sent forward by Lord Conway to watch their motions. There was no plundering or devastation, as in the invasions of other days; but, according to a writer who served under Leslie, "the camp-fires of the Scots so terrified the country-people that they fled with bag and baggage towards the south, leaving their desolate houses to the mercie of the armie." Marching in three divisions, six miles apart, the first led by General Leslie, the second by Lord Almond, and the third by Major-General Baillie, they were joined by a division of 7,000 Scots who had entered England by the Kelso route; and thus reinforced, with the poor peasantry flying before them, they advanced to the beautiful plain called Middleton Haugh.

Thence they marched again, with their artillery in front, and their flanks covered by cavalry; and crossing the Coquet on the 25th, halted at Nether Witton, where the woods furnished them with abundance of fuel; and on the 27th the advanced guard, under the Earl of Montrose, came in sight of Newcastle, which was then garrisoned, according to some English writers, by 3,000 horse and 5,000 foot, with a great train of artillery; but according to Strafford's defence of himself before the English Parliament, there were 14,000 horse and foot in the town on the 24th day of August.

Halting where the road branches off to Newburn Ford, at the distance of four miles from Newcastle, Leslie sent the drum-major of Lord Montgomerie's regiment, with letters to the governor and mayor, demanding leave to march freely through the town. The governor was Sir Jacob Astley (afterwards Lord Astley, of Reading), who had served in Holland under Sir Francis Vere, and was afterwards sergeant-major-general of the Royal troops at Edgehill and Newbury. He returned the letters to the drum-major unopened, saying, "Make my service to your general, and inform him that if he sends any more sealed letters here, their bearer will find that he had better have stayed at home" (Rushworth).

Leslie knew Astley well, as they had been comrades together in Bohemia; and, supposing that there might be sharp work in attempting to storm Newcastle, he resolved to force the passage of the Tyne at Newburn Ford, and with the Earl of Montrose still leading the advanced guard, he wheeled off in that direction. Immediately below the little villages lies the ford referred to. There the Lord Conway had taken every measure to dispute the passage of the river, by the erection of redoubts planted with twelve pieces of cannon, and of breastworks lined by 3,000 picked musketeers, in rear of whom were stationed 2,500 horse. A dispatch from the Earl of Strafford reached him, with orders to repel at all hazards any attempt of the Scots to pass the stream, as the king was advancing with all speed. On the other hand, Leslie, supposing he was far off, and being resolved to move warily, after a careful reconnaissance encamped, but issued orders for the storming of the English works at daybreak. That evening a Scottish officer, well-mounted, with a large plume in his bonnet, had the temerity to water his horse in the Tyne, and while doing so was shot dead.

In military talent, activity, and skill, no man in Britain then - unless we except Cromwell - was equal to Sir Alexander Leslie. That night he had cannon slung to the top of Newburn church tower; he placed nine pieces of Colonel Hamilton's train in ambush, among some copsewood near the river; while several companies of musketeers quietly and silently lined all the available garden walls, cottages, windows, and hedgerows on the northern side of the ford, the attack on which commenced at daybreak.

The English elevated their steel caps and plumed beavers on the points of their weapons, and received the first fire of the Scots with cheers of derision, which were a little premature, for in three minutes the river's banks became ablaze with musketry, and were enveloped in smoke. The Scottish battery from the ambush slew many of the enemy; its fire was directed unexpectedly on the redoubts, while the gunners there were labouring to dislodge the Scots from Newburn steeple. Leslie's train, being under skilled officers, beat down an English redoubt, in which the infantry mutinied against Colonel Lunsford and their officers; and on one particularly well-directed shot falling among them, they fled, leaving behind twenty killed and a great many wounded.

"Immediately on this, General Leslie sent forward his Life Guards, the Regiment of the College of Justice. This was a nobly-accoutred corps, led by Sir Thomas Hope, of Kerse. Major Ballantyne, with sixteen volunteers, led the way across the river. Then the Earls of Crawford and Loudon, each at the head of his regiment, with colours waving, and drums beating the "Scots March," advanced to the ford, under cover of the masked battery and a few field-pieces which now opened upon the English reserve drawn up on the little plain beyond the stream. When this movement took place, Lord Conway's trumpets instantly sounded a retreat; the English gunners drew off their cannon, and followed their fugitive infantry. Then the Scottish troops, in heavy columns, passed the river in full force, Montrose, Queensberry, Dalhousie, and other lords, each at the head of his regiment. Several of the English musketeers, who had not time to abandon the sconces, were taken prisoners; but the best and bravest of their troops had yet to be encountered" ("Memoirs of Montrose," 1858).

Passage of Newburn Ford.

209

These were the horse, a body of gentlemen and cavaliers of high birth and lofty spirit, all splendidly mounted, and brilliantly armed and accoutred. They were led by Sir John Digby; Ferdinando, Lord Fairfax, of Cameron; and Henry, Lord Wilmot, the Sergeant-Major-General of the Cavalry, afterwards first Earl of Rochester.

On passing to the front through the streets of Newcastle on the preceding day, all these wild spirits are described as having ridden in great disorder, brandishing their swords, waving their plumed beavers, drinking at every other door to the health of the king, swearing that they would "fight to the last gasp, and to exterminate each at least a dozen of Scots."

In no way discouraged by the flight of their fugitive musketeers, whom they taunted as "the scum of London," closing up in twelve squadrons in a narrow place between two thick hedgerows, they made a charge so heavy and furious on the Scottish Life Guards, that, despite all the valour of Sir Thomas Hope, his troopers began to recoil on each other; but being pressed forward by the rear squadrons, they were forced to the front, and a dreadful struggle with rapier and pistol ensued. Being all gentlemen, no man would yield an inch on either side, and all seemed equally ready to die on the spot; but it was the very madness of courage for a mere handful of cavalry to attempt to dispute the progress of an entire army.

A royal standard of England, being that of Lord Conway's own troop, was taken, and the bearer, Charles Porter, was killed by a pistol-shot. Sir John Digby, Lord Wilmot, Sergeant-Major O'Niel, and many more, were unhorsed, disarmed, and taken prisoners; "while many gallant Scottish gentlemen were shot, run through, or trod down beneath the swaying mass of horsemen, who dashed their ranks against each other like two living floods in that narrow alley."

Among those who fell were Thomas Dauling and Cornet

Macghie of Leslie's Dragoons [son of Sir Patrick Macghie, of Larg, in Galloway), who was killed by his father's side.

On receiving a flank fire from 1,000 musketeers under Colonels Ramsay and Blair, the English horse gave way in irretrievable confusion, and fled to Newcastle, leaving all their officers, with eighty prisoners, and forty slain and more wounded, in the hands of Leslie, who for that night bivouacked at Ryetown.

The routed cavaliers threw away their arms, which were gleaned up next day by the Scottish foragers; and while galloping through Newcastle they scared the inhabitants by crying, "Fye! fye! for guides to Durham. Now, man, woman, and child, pack up and begone, for those naked devils, the Scots, are upon you!"

Leslie had very few killed; and the English loss is so uncertain that Clarendon states it to be twelve, while Whitelock gives it at 300 killed, wounded, and taken, and others at 300 killed. The dead were properly interred by the Scots; and on the first appearance of an accommodation, the prisoners were courteously dismissed.

The "Scots March," referred to when Leslie's troops advanced to the ford, was a peculiar beat on the drum, used as lately as 1818, by the City Guard of Edinburgh. There was also a similar cadence on the drum used in the sister country, known as the "English March," which is thus mentioned in a warrant of Charles I, issued at Westminster in the seventh year of his reign (1632), as, "the march of this our English nation, so famous in all the honourable atchievements and glorious warres of this our kingdom in forraigne parts, which, thorough the negligence and carelessness of drummers, and by long discontinuance, was so altered and changed from the ancient gravitie and majesty thereof, as it was in danger utterly to have been lost and forgotten. It pleased our late deare brother, Prince Henry, to revive and rectify the same, by ordaining the establishment

211

of one certayne measure, which was beaten in his presence at Greenwich in 1610;" and this measure, continues the warrant, is to be used in future by "all drummers within our Kingdom of England and Principalitie of Wales."

Notwithstanding all his boasting, Sir Jacob Astley, with his garrison, deserted from Newcastle on the approach of General Leslie, who entered it first at the head of the Life Guards, attended by the Lords Montrose and Almond; the mayor, Sir Peter Ridale, with the aldermen, receiving them at the bridge bareheaded, with every sign of outward respect to conceal their real dislike. Leslie posted guards everywhere, seized all the artillery, 5,000 stand of arms, all the vast stores collected for the troops of the king, together with four large ships laden with corn for his cavalry. "Though elated by their success, the soldiers preserved the most rigid and exact discipline, abstained from all plunder, and rigidly paid for everything received from the burgesses; and, being anxious to gain over to their interests the Puritans of England in general, and those of London in particular, the Scottish general, on seizing Tynemouth and Shields, wrote to the Lord Mayor, informing him that, being aware how necessary for its comfort was the traffic in coals that 'though he had taken the places whence it was almost solely embarked for the Thames, its transmission would not be interrupted'; tidings which, as the Covenanters cunningly anticipated, had the effect of raising among the Londoners loud praises of their clemency, and a clamour in their favour."

The Earl of Lothian was made governor, with a garrison of 2,000 men, and the Earl of Dunfermline's brigade seized Durham. At these events the rage of Strafford knew no bounds; he ordered the cattle to be everywhere driven south through Yorkshire, all millstones to be broken or buried, and the supplies everywhere to be cut off.

Daily now the king saw the folly of meddling with the affairs of the Scots, and that the presence of their army was becoming useful to the English malcontents. An accommodation was arrived at, and England was to pay the expenses of the war. Among these, "Scotland estimated the loss of her trade at £50,000; 500 vessels stopped on the seas by English warships; £7,000 odd for fortifying the castle of Edinburgh; £100,000 for losses occasioned to nobles and burghs; 1,000 horses for officers' baggage; the expenses of the (extra) regiments of Munro, Home, Argyle, Marischal, Sinclair, and others, which would not have been required, with necessary fortifications, and for ships sunk in the Clyde to bar out the English fleet; and as nothing was undercharged, the sum-total was certainly enormous" ("Memoirs of Montrose").

As England delayed payment of the last instalment, the Scottish Estates threatened to occupy her border counties with 3,000 horse and 10,000 foot; and ultimately it was settled that both armies should be disbanded on the 6th of August, 1641. But the Scots retained in pay the regiments of Lord Sinclair, Cochrane, and Munro, as the nucleus of another army for the wars which they foresaw were to come.

MORE FROM THE SAME SERIES

Most books from the 'Military History from Original Sources' series are edited and endorsed by Emmy Award winning film maker and military historian Bob Carruthers, producer of Discovery Channel's Line of Fire and Weapons of War and BBC's Both Sides of the Line. Long experience and strong editorial control gives the military history enthusiast the ability to buy with confidence. The series advisor is David McWhinnie, producer of the acclaimed Battlefield series for Discovery Channel. David and Bob have co-produced books and films with a wide variety of the UK's leading historians including Professor John Erickson and Dr David Chandler.
Where possible the books draw on rare primary sources to give the military enthusiast new insights into a fascinating subject.

The English Civil Wars	The Zulu Wars	Into Battle with Napoleon 1812	Waterloo 1815
The Anglo-Saxon Chronicle	Medieval Warfare	Renaissance Warfare	1914-1918
Sea Battles in the Age of Sail	Sun Tzu - The Art of War	Recollections of the Great War in the Air	Soldier of the Empire

For more information visit www.pen-and-sword.co.uk